Planning and implementing successful system migrations

Planning and implementing successful system migrations

Edited by

Graeme Muirhead
Bibliographic Database Manager
Solihull Education, Libraries & Arts

LIBRARY ASSOCIATION PUBLISHING
LONDON

Published by
Library Association Publishing
7 Ridgmount Street
London WC1E 7AE

Library Association Publishing is wholly owned by The Library Association.

First published 1997

British Library Cataloguing in Publication Data

A catalogue record for this book is available from the British Library.

ISBN 1-85604-218-9

The system migrations described in this book show libraries and information services in the process of changing from closed, proprietary library management systems to open systems, so-called third generation systems. Any comparisons between the products which are being replaced and the new products are not comparisons of the specific systems but of the generations of computer systems to which the particular systems belong. Nothing in this book should be taken as a criticism or endorsement of any system supplier or their products and services.

Typeset in 10/12pt Aldine and 12/14pt Zurich by Library Association Publishing. Printed and made in Great Britain by Bookcraft (Bath) Ltd.

Contents

Acknowledgments

The editor would like to thank the following groups and individuals for their assistance, without which this book would not have been possible:

The contributors for undertaking the difficult and at times sensitive task of writing about migrating to a new system
Carole Burton, Interlibrary Loans Assistant, Solihull Education, Libraries and Arts Department
Andrew Cranfield and Carsten Dibbern of Dansk Data Elektronik A/S
Frances Richardson of BLCMP Library Services Ltd
Chris MacArthur, Systems Administrator, Southampton Institute of Higher Education
Kate Clark, Barbara Thompson and Sarah Coulter, Solihull Schools Library Service
Meg Gain, National Council for Educational Technology
The School Library Association
The staff of Library Association Publishing

Contributors

Janet Broome Project Manager, Ameritech Library Services, UK

Jan Condon Librarian, Solihull Sixth Form College

Mark Evans International Technical Support Programmer, Ameritech Library Services, USA

George Geddes Systems Librarian, Jordanhill Library

Barry Hickman Systems Librarian, Coventry City Libraries

Vibeke Hvidtfeldt Head Librarian, Slagelse Centralbibliotek, Denmark

Ruth Jenkinson Head, Learning Resource Centre, Edge Hill University College

Chris Lowe Systems Librarian, Edge Hill University College

Aksel G. Mikkelsen Librarian and Computer Coordinator, Slagelse Centralbibliotek, Denmark

Graeme Muirhead Bibliographic Database Manager, Solihull Education, Libraries and Arts Department

Dennis Nicholson Head of Library Systems, Strathclyde University Library

Guenever Pachent Assistant Director, Suffolk Libraries & Heritage

Steve Penn Project Manager, BLCMP

Douglas Reed Service Manager, Professional Resources, Suffolk Libraries & Heritage

Jenny Rowley Head of School, Management and Social Sciences, Edge Hill University College

John Scott Cree Senior Librarian, Customer Services (London), Department of Health

Jean Shaw Deputy Head of Library Systems, Strathclyde University Library

Acronyms and abbreviations

AACR	Anglo-American Cataloguing Rules
ALS	Automated Library Systems Ltd
ANSI	American National Standards Institute
ASCII	American Standard Code for Information Interchange
ATM	asynchronous transfer mode
BIBS	BIBlioteks System
BIDS	Bath Information and Data Services
BLAISE	British Library Automated Information Service
BLCMP	Birmingham Libraries Cooperative Mechanization Project (now BLCMP Library Services Ltd)
BLDSC	British Library Document Supply Centre
BNB	British National Bibliography
BNF	British Nuclear Fuels
BRS	Bibliographic Retrieval Service
BT	British Telecom
BUBL	Bulletin Board for Libraries
CAIRS	Computer Assisted Information Retrieval System
CATRIONA	Cataloguing and Retrieval of Information over Networks Applications
CCTA	Central Computer and Telecommunications Agency
CD	compact disc
CD-ROM	compact disc-read only memory
CLSI	Computer Library Services International
CoFHE	Colleges of Further and Higher Education Group of The Library Association
COM	computer output on microfiche
CPI	Capital Planning Information
CPU	central processing unit
CWIS	campus-wide information service, or community-wide information service
DDE	Dansk Data Elektronik
DH	Department of Health
DHSS	Department of Health and Social Security
DIMS	Document and Information Management Strategy
DoE	Department of the Environment
DOS	disk operating system
DSS	Department of Social Security
EARL	Electronic Access to Resources in Libraries
EC	European Community (now European Union)
ECCTIS	Educational Counselling and Credit Transfer Information System

EDI	electronic data interchange
e-mail	electronic mail
FE	further education
FM	facilities management
FTE	full-time equivalent (staff)
FTP	file transfer protocol
GB	Gigabyte
GNVQ	General National Vocational Qualification
GUI	graphical user interface
HMSO	Her Majesty's Stationery Office
ILL	interlibrary loans
IIS	Institute of Information Scientists
ISDN	integrated service digital network
ISO	International Standards Organization
IT	information technology
JANET	Joint Academic Network
JMLS	John Menzies Library Supply
KB	Kilobytes
KWIRS	Key Words Information Retrieval System
LA	Library Association
LAN	local-area network
LEA	local education authority
LOCAS	local cataloguing service
LIS	library and information services
LMS	local management of schools
MARC	machine-readable cataloguing
MB	Megabyte
MHz	Megahertz
MIS	management information system
NHS	National Health Service
NHSME	National Health Service Management Executive
NISS	National Information on Software and Services
OCLC	Online Computer Library Center
OCS	open computing systems
OPAC	online public access catalogue
OR	operational requirement
OSI	open systems interconnection
PAC	public access catalogue
PC	personal computer
PERT	programme evaluation and review technique
PIN	personal identification number
PRINCE	projects in controlled environments
PSS	packet switch stream
RAID	random array of inexpensive disks

RAM	random access memory
RDBMS	relational database management system
RFP	request for proposal
SALSER	Scottish Academic Libraries' Serials
SCOLCAP	Scottish Library Cooperative Automation Project
SDI	selective dissemination of information
SIMS	Schools Information Management System
SIR	Schools Information Retrieval
SISP	strategic information-systems planning, strategic information-systems plan
SJVLS	San Joaquin Valley Library System
SLA	service level agreement
SLG	School Libraries Group of The Library Association
SNI	Siemens-Nixdorf
SOUR	statement of user requirement
SQL	structured query language
SSFC	Solihull Sixth Form College
SWOT	strengths, weaknesses, opportunities, threats
TCP/IP	transmission control protocol/Internet protocol
UCCA	Universities Central Council on Admissions
UDC	Universal Decimal Classification
UKOP	United Kingdom Official Publications
UTP	untwisted pair (cable)
VT	virtual terminal
WAIS	wide-area information server
WAN	wide-area network
WWW	World Wide Web

Introduction

Graeme Muirhead

New technology – new mindsets

The extensive computerization of libraries and information centres in the 1970s and 1980s invites superlatives. Quantum leap, revolution, paradigm shift, the dawn of a new era – library automation was certainly all of these things. The new possibilities offered by computer-based systems were embraced enthusiastically by the library and information profession, but the information technology (IT) revolution was not a bloodless one. The introduction of new technology sometimes led to resistance or resentment among staff at an operational level, and in many cases systems were undersized or proved to be functionally inadequate in some way.

With hindsight we can see that adopting the new technologies was the easy part of the process. It has taken longer for organizations to change their culture and nurture the new skills necessary for the successful management and exploitation of these technologies.

Part of this collective learning experience has been the realization in libraries and information centres that automation, far from being a one-off project, is an on-going process. The cyclical migration to new systems is a fact of life. Libraries or information centres which began experimenting with computer applications in the 1970s are probably now on their third or fourth system. Few of the libraries which bought their first integrated library system in the early to mid-1980s have still to migrate to a third generation system. Few library and information workers have not seen their jobs radically changed by the introduction of computerization; many have made a career of library automation, as library system managers, as analysts or programmers with a library system vendor, or as consultants. Both libraries and system suppliers have acquired a wealth of experience from migrating to new systems. One aim of this book is to uncover and share some of this knowledge.

The term 'migration' can mean various things in the context of computerized systems. Migration has been defined as 'the process of changing or significantly upgrading automated library systems',[1] and 'the evolutionary process that bridges one system to the next'.[2] These definitions underline the point made above, namely the open-ended nature of migration: automation as a process rather than a project.

At a more practical level, migration can involve:

- moving from one hardware platform to another
- changing the application software, remaining with the same vendor or switching to a completely different product from another supplier
- changing operating system, programming language or database management system
- network and telecommunications changes, for example replacing analogue lines with digital lines.

Most of the migration case studies in this book entailed changing all of these system components.

Migrating systems – migrating users

It is important to say that migration is about moving data *and users*. Automation is fundamental to service delivery. It is so highly visible to staff and customers that minimal changes in functionality can have far reaching and disproportionate effects. At the same time it is so pervasive as to be taken for granted – until there is downtime. As a consequence, the importance of 'people issues' during migration and for the successful operation of a new system cannot be overstated: 'The full potential of any system can not be realized without making human resources development the top priority of the library administration'.[3] In addition to disruption during the changeover (physical disruption during the installation of new hardware and cabling, adapting to new software functionality and changes in workflow, etc.), system migration can sometimes require a deeper cultural shift. For example, this may involve moving away from paper-based communication and learning to use electronic mail (e-mail) and groupware; or learning to conceptualize the library not only as a physical space and the library system as a closed, self-contained system but more in terms of the digital networked library providing access rather than holdings, information 'just in time' rather than 'just in case'.

Change on the scale of a system migration will inevitably cause varying levels of stress for all concerned. It is often said that four of the most traumatic life events in the late twentieth century are bereavement, divorce, moving house and changing jobs. Perhaps changing systems should be added to this list. Like all of these events, system migration can be an opportunity for a fresh start, but like them it too means change, uncertainty and separation. 'Technostress' can manifest itself in a range of physical and psychological symptoms – anxiety, denial, panic, mental fatigue, intolerance, physical pain or discomfort, absenteeism, and so on – which may affect an employee's job performance, interpersonal relations and general well-being.[4] Some of the most common reasons for technostress in the context of a system migration are

- loss of control of the work environment
- uncertainty about how the job will change, or if there will be a job at all
- fear that skills acquired over several years will become worthless

- anxiety about an increase in workload or the inability to keep up with the pace of change
- loss of status
- potential disruption of interpersonal relations and 'comfort zones'.

A fundamental goal in any system migration must be minimizing the negative aspects of the change and accentuating the positive.[5] The case studies presented here show how this can be achieved by using the following methods:

- **Consultation** Wide consultation during the needs assessment and staff participation in decision-making will prevent feelings of lack of control and ensure a commitment to success on the part of all staff.
- **Communication** Communicating the purpose and aims of the proposed change and the benefits it will bring, and keeping staff informed of progress (or lack of progress) on timescales, for example, by providing regular information bulletins.
- **Phased implementation** This will reduce the impact of change on those involved, ensure adequate time to test functionality and data conversion, and deliver training in a controlled manner.
- **Training** Training requirements will vary from institution to institution, but, in general, training should be hands-on, delivered within the actual working environment, timely, not rushed and on-going.
- **Documentation** Good documentation will reduce some of the uncertainty about the new system. Vendor documentation will almost certainly need to be rewritten in language comprehensible by nontechnical staff and using real examples that are relevant to the local library.
- **Planning** Planning underpins all these measures. There must be sufficient time to consult and train, a clear migration path so that staff can measure progress and a contingency plan if things go wrong. For large-scale computer projects, the PRINCE (projects in controlled environments) methodology might be considered.[6] However, project planning can be facilitated by using much simpler methods such as a Gantt charts or network analysis, e.g. critical path analysis and PERT (programme evaluation and review technique), or appropriate project management software, e.g. Microsoft *Project* or Computer Associates' *Super project*.[7]

Migrate or stagnate

For many libraries and information services the realization that their system will not last forever has come as something of a rude awakening. The lifecycle of a system will be influenced by many factors: the pace of new developments in technology; the dynamics of the computer systems market; the needs of the user community; the availability of funding and competing demands to spend in areas other than automation; organizational politics and changes in central and local government policy. Libraries and information centres can either anticipate these developments and so become self-determining, or they can react to them. There are many published accounts of 'forced' migrations in which 'push' factors have been the main reason for the acquisition of a replacement system. These push factors include unacceptable response times, costly maintenance on obsolescent hardware, dissatisfaction with software support, lack of vendor support for old products and vendor takeovers/insolvency. Because such migrations are usually reactions to unforeseen events, there is unlikely to be an overall plan and there will be insufficient time for the migration. In these circumstances, it is more likely that the library or information centre will be at the mercy of the supplier and may not fully comprehend the various stages of the migration and their implications.

For other libraries and information services the 'pull' of a new system better able to meet the organization's business objectives is the dominant cause of the migration. In recent years, we have seen a generational shift in library and information systems. Newly developed products are usually referred to as third generation systems. Third generation systems are so-called 'open' systems based on the adoption of industry-wide standards. To be truly open, systems need to be standardized in two distinct areas. One set of standards refers to the way computer systems communicate with each other: OSI (Open Systems Interconnection) is the seven-layer reference model developed the by ISO (International Standards Organization), but this has been overtaken by the more widely used TCP/IP (Transmission Control Protocol/Internet Protocol) used on the Internet and elsewhere. The second area of standardization covers the components of the computer system itself – operating system, RDBMS (relational database management system), programming language and so on – and systems which are compatible in these areas are termed open computing systems (OCS).[8]

The potential benefits of a third generation library system include

- faster processing and greater reliability based on low-cost, reliable, high performance hardware and client/server architecture
- access to wide-area networks (interoperability)
- better management information
- more user-friendly front ends, often Web-like graphical user interfaces with hypertext links
- 'vertical, horizontal and forward portability' – the ease with which data and programs can be carried to smaller or larger computers or to a computer from a different supplier[9]
- a shorter development cycle for new functionality.

The experience of many libraries and information centres, however, is that basic functionality to match that achieved by second generation systems has been slow to be developed, often being given lower priority by system vendors than more eye-catching features such as Web OPACs (online public access catalogues); and that the promised freedom to choose their preferred hardware platform is usually quite restricted.

The steps involved in a migration project are similar to those involved in first time automation, namely

- needs, assessment and system specification
- planning and executing the procurement process
- data migration
- site preparation and hardware installation
- training and documentation
- testing and evaluating new system performance.

Although the basic steps are the same, there are also the following significant differences:

- With successive migrations, there is likely to be a development of experience on the part of library and information workers, leading to better specifications, more confidence during negotiations with vendors, firmer contracts, better planning and management of every stage of the project, and more realistic expectations about the system they will actually get.
- Staff and customer experience for better or worse of the previous system. System end-users are able to contribute valuable expertise to the needs assessment and selection processes, and they often have greater insight into practical issues than library administrators or system managers. When training in the new system is delivered, staff who have experience of one automation system should have a conceptual framework to enable them to learn the new system more quickly.
- The first migration from one automated system to another is in some ways as novel as a first time automation project (e.g. migrating data between systems is very different from creating a database in machine-readable format) and it too will contribute to the pool of experience available in future migrations.
- 'Meta evaluation' or 'evaluating the evaluation process'[10] is a set of measures which recognize the value of learning from migration experience. In practice, meta evaluation means that planning must include measures of success and post-implementation time to analyse the overall performance. Meta evaluation also requires that the project is documented for future reference (a valuable safeguard against the departure of key staff).
- Finally, system suppliers too have learned from the migration experience. Although every migration is unique, it is now a common enough occurrence for all the major players to have developed data conversion programs and to have finely tuned project methodologies based on their experience of performing many other migrations.

It is hoped that the case studies presented in this volume will make some of this hard-earned experience available more widely and that this will aid those who will be migrating in the coming years.

The case studies approach

When planning this book, it was felt that a case studies approach would be valuable. The case studies approach is eminently suited to the subject of the book in that it can be seen as an extension of the standard procurement process which often includes site visits, networking among colleagues, and other methods of exchanging information. Moreover, case studies are popular with information professionals because they

- fuse theory and practice
- have a loose narrative structure
- have a 'people element'
- present real-life scenarios with all that that implies in terms of conflict resolution, problem solving, complexity, etc.

The case studies presented in this volume were chosen in accordance with the following criteria:

- they must be recent – that is occurring within the past two to three years
- they must be representative of a cross-section of types of institutions – public libraries, academic libraries, special and government libraries, school and college libraries
- they must be international in scope
- they should represent a variety of library systems and system suppliers
- the migrations should vary in size and complexity.

Other key points which contributors were asked to address were that

- they should not only provide factual information and descriptions of the technical aspects of hardware and software, the problems (if any) of data conversion and the logistics of implementation, but they should also deal with the in some ways less predictable 'people issues'
- they should attempt to analyse the ways in which their migration was different from first time automation: What did they do well? What would they do differently? What are the lessons for others?

The examples chosen for this casebook also have in common the fact that they were all highly visible migrations in that the new system, whether from a new supplier or not, made available new functionality requiring adaptation on the part of staff and users. The migrations presented here were all highly complex operations which took place at a number of levels, involved the successful replacement of the numerous hardware and software components that make up any system, and required the coordination and management of many participants over a period of months and sometimes years. If, as was suggested earlier, migration is a necessary process, it seems equally inevitable that such a complex undertaking will rarely be trouble free. An important part of the brief to contributors was that such difficulties and problems were not to be glossed over. Although every migration story is in one sense unique, it is always possible to extract lessons which can be generalized and made transferable to other circumstances. Given the potential political and commercial sensitivity surrounding such a request it is to the credit of the libraries and information services which have contributed to the volume, and indeed the system suppliers who have supported them, that they have made this information public.

The original plan was for a series of chapters following an identical structure. The main reason for this was that it would make it easier for readers to compare migrations in widely varying organizations. However, it soon became apparent that this would not work. Although migrations follow similar patterns, there are many unique local circumstances which make it difficult to impose a rigorous structure. For example, some migrations are very problematic from the point of view of data conversion, whereas for others there is virtually nothing to say under this heading. Similarly for training or staff acceptance of the new system. So a rigid, externally imposed structure would prevent the authors from saying what they want to say and force them to try to say something when in fact they have nothing to say. Finally, to have seven or eight chapters with the same headings would probably be quite monotonous for readers. For these reasons, the original plan was abandoned in favour of a freer structure.

Chapter outline

Chapter 1
In this chapter, Jenkinson, Lowe and Rowley examine a variety of information systems methodologies and illustrate these with reference to an actual migration project carried out in a medium-sized college library at Edge Hill University College. The chapter deals specifically with three approaches: hard systems methodologies, strategies for the management of change and SISP (strategic information systems planning), with the aim of contributing to the identification of the features of a methodology to support systems migration. Although the main systems migration project described in the chapter was successful, a subsequent software upgrade project presented its own problems. The chapter concludes that systems migration is a learning experience in the management change that embraces both systems and people.

Chapter 2
Chapter 2 describes Suffolk County Libraries & Heritage's recent migration to third generation systems. Suffolk's approach to selection contained four significant features: 'the requirement for a third generation system at a time when they were at the very early stages of development; a generalized specification couched in terms of outcomes, not detailed functionality; a requirement for an information network and for archive cataloguing functions as well as for the tra-

ditional library housekeeping system; and an evaluation process which included demonstrations in libraries by the systems suppliers to the public . . . and the testing of software on site'. Suffolk's insistence on a third generation system at a time when such systems were still relatively untried has paid important dividends. For example, the use of industry-standard products, RDBMS and a fourth generation language (4GL) have decreased the time taken by the system supplier to develop new functionality and TCP/IP has enabled Libraries & Heritage to integrate into the County Council's corporate network providing e-mail, word-processing and access to council and other information for even the smallest branch. Pachent and Reed focus on a number of unique characteristics which have enabled Suffolk to turn vision into reality: community involvement in the selection and evaluation of the new system, the role of the library network in bringing together a geographically dispersed rural community and staff, and the role of museums and archive staff and how the library system accommodates their needs.

Chapter 3

Strathclyde University Library went out to tender for a new library system in 1995 shortly after the University had merged with Jordanhill College. Nicholson, Shaw and Geddes describe pre-merger automation in both institutions and the move to Dynix Horizon – a project which meant in effect replacing two systems, a database merge and the implementation of a new automation and networking strategy – from the standpoint of the library systems staff. The scale and complexity of the changes almost inevitably led to slippages in the original timescales in several areas. The chapter demonstrates the need for clear and unambiguous agreements between libraries and system suppliers, the benefits of having a project manager who has an insider's understanding of library and information work, and how seemingly intractable problems can be overcome by a partnership approach.

Chapter 4

In this chapter Evans relates a double migration on a similar scale to that described in Chapter 3, this time from the standpoint of the system vendor. The San Joaquin Valley Library System (SJVLS) is located in California and is a consortium of seven counties with over 100 individual libraries. Prior to Dynix (their current system), four of the counties were using a Ulisys system and three others were using an LS2 system. Due to financial and political constraints, the two groups decided to merge. This chapter describes the rationale behind data conversion and hardware installation methodologies and demonstrates the benefits of an incremental transfer from one system to another. Evans also provides examples of the kinds of practical problems that can arise during a database conversion (and merge in this case) and shows how these were overcome.

Chapter 5

The Department of Health (DH) has a mature office information system which links approximately 5500 staff in multiple sites across the country giving access to a variety of products including e-mail, word-processing, spreadsheets, desktop publishing and statistical/financial modelling packages. The chapter focuses on aspects of the project to manage implementation in 1995 of Sirsi's Unicorn integrated library system on this large network with multiple applications. Concurrent with the Unicorn implementation, work was in progress elsewhere in the DH to put up a press index service, a Hansard summary service and electronic directory of business as well as on-going efforts to network successfully CD-ROMs. Among other things, the chapter illustrates in a very practical way how the vendor response to a tender may not always mean what it says and the importance of having an experienced project manager to oversee the procurement process. While fully endorsing the need to consult staff at all times, Scott Cree recommends careful management of user expectations for a smooth migration.

Chapter 6

This chapter provides an experience of migration from another member country of the European Union (EU). The Danish company DDE (Dansk Data Elektronik), was the brainchild of four young engineers who in the mid-1970s started working with the first generation of microprocessors. Together they founded a company that today provides a range of systems and services to customers in countries throughout Europe and beyond based on its Supermax range of computers. The first library to sign a contract with DDE was Herning Central Library in 1988 and by the time Slagelse Central Library, which is the focus of this case study, chose DDE, the company had more than 75 public library customers. In this chapter, Hvidtfeldt and Mikkelsen analyse the migration from a Swedish system called BIBS (BIBlioteks System) to DDE's 'library solution'. Like the UK, Denmark has a long tradition of providing free public libraries, but Danish libraries have quite unique automation requirements which many of the systems available in the UK and the USA cannot yet meet. Despite these differences, the Slagelse experience reinforces the lessons of other libraries with respect to the need for thorough market research, staff involvement, well-timed training, etc., and demonstrates how mistakes made during earlier phases of automation can be avoided in the future. Slagelse's migration also shows how despite all the planning, there can still be an element of sheer good luck in making a migration successful – in this case a former deputy librarian had been promoted to the post of IT manager within the Council's administration and was therefore able to ensure that library interests were fully represented at negotiations with suppliers.

Chapter 7

School and college libraries have needs and priorities that are in many respects different from those of the large and medium-sized services that have been the subject of the other chapters. Often professional isolation, lack of status and lack of expertise can combine to create a barrier to automating the school or college library. This is not the case with Solihull Sixth Form College (SSFC). The college library is unusual among libraries of a similar kind in that it is in the process of migrating to its second system. Since it was established in 1974, the college has shown a willingness to lead the way in introducing a range of new technologies and so this chapter shows how a synergy developed between automated library management systems and various other computer-based applications. One major factor in the success of SSFC's automation over the years has been the college librarian's use of networking skills, lobbying and enlisting the support of management and teaching staff, consulting library staff, and drawing on the IT skills and experience of others, internally and externally. Perhaps these strategies should be a part of all migrations, but they are crucial in small or one-person libraries of all kinds.

Chapter 8

Relationships between library and information services and library system vendors have been difficult at times: information professionals and computing professionals, public service values and the marketplace – there was bound to be friction. Over the years, we have seen a greater mutual understanding between these two groups. Librarians have learned a great deal about computer technology, computer system suppliers have begun to listen to their customers and publicly-funded bodies such as libraries have increasingly been exposed to the same marketplace economics that drive system suppliers. In the 1990s the emphasis is on partnership and collaboration, with, for example, libraries directly involved in designing and testing new software, and system vendors participating in library-based research projects. This chapter exemplifies just such an approach as applied to the migration process. In part one, Hickman, from the viewpoint of the systems librarian, describes how Coventry City Libraries moved from a CLSI system to BLCMP's Talis system. In part two, Penn reports on how the project was managed by BLCMP and what the company learned from the experience. The Coventry migration involved a number of risks. Fortunately, none of them materialized, but it is worth making the point that the risks were identified and the responsibility for them clearly defined – this is a sure way to avoid recriminations if things do go wrong.

Chapter 9

In this chapter, Broome highlights some of the elements that go towards the 'perfect migration', drawing on her experience in posts in libraries and with system suppliers and consultants. This chapter reiterates that libraries and system suppliers must work together as partners and likens this relationship to a marriage, which can only work if there are realistic expectations and flexibility on both sides. Other necessary ingredients for a perfect migration are realistic and achievable project milestones with a fall-back position if things slip, a sense of proportion ('there is little point in making a drama out of a minor problem'), adequate resourcing by both parties and sufficient time to test the data conversion.

Conclusions

If the evidence provided by these case histories is typical, as a profession we have learned a great deal about the technical aspects of implementing new systems. But the most noticeable progress has been in the 'softer' aspects of computerization and the management of change – consulting and involving staff in the decision-making process, and communicating with all system users throughout the process of change.

However, two areas still need to be addressed satisfactorily by many institutions: the economic aspects of migration and the need for new skills in an open systems, multivendor environment.

The economics of system migration

Despite the rise of the 'library without walls', for most library and information services the local library management system is still of fundamental importance for the delivery of core services. It supports most of the basic business areas and, without it, staff would not be able to perform their duties. On top of this, the library system represents an enormous financial investment – probably the biggest budget item after staff and library stock. These costs are summed up well in a recent CPI (Capital Planning Information) publication:

> In terms of larger academic and public systems a system budget of £1 million is not untypical. The overall 'cost of ownership' of such a system over five years will be two to three times the purchase cost. [*Software maintenance at 15% and hardware maintenance at 10–12% p.a. will amount to another 60–70% over 5 years, training and (usually hidden) learning costs will add another significant amount, and there will be various software and hardware upgrades.*]
>
> The library service itself will be costing several £million each year, and although much of this is not directly related to the computer system, the latter will be a key factor in how well the service is delivered and the public's perception of the service they are getting (with their money). A library service costing say £5m each year will cost £25 million over the projected five year life of our proposed new system. A 1% improvement in value for money is therefore notionally worth £250,000 and even a 0.1% difference would be worth £25,000.[11]

It is vital that this investment is properly managed. All too often, however, library managers have been forced (often through no fault of their own) to resort to short-termism and opportunism. Too often libraries have been rushed into replacing their system or have tended to regard the replacement of a computer system as a major, one-off capital expense with no allowance for depreciation or increasing maintenance costs as equipment ages. Library managers and their parent institutions urgently need to face up to the reality that automation is an on-going investment and plan accordingly.

> I . . . think institutions will need to take a much more evolutionary approach to IT investment. The pace of technological change, and the pace of change in user requirements, are now both so rapid that the idea of a five or seven year life cycle for a system is obsolete. Systems must be able to grow and change organically, and the development of open systems, and of more distributed approaches to the provision of processing power, make that possible. Institutions need to adjust their financial planning accordingly.[12]

Libraries and information services which have made the big leap from closed, proprietary systems to open systems and which have migrated their data to relational models should find that incremental change is possible until the next major technological revolution (whenever that happens). This approach will enable them to spread costs and respond flexibly to new expectations from users and new developments in technology. Equally important, it will address the human (and organizational) need of staff for continuity. The 'paradox of change' is that 'the constant state of change needed for an organization's wellbeing is itself dependent on the organization's internal stability'.[13] By reducing the impact of change and by habituating staff to regular but small-scale changes, incremental change is a strategy that can achieve the necessary balance.

One fairly obvious final point. The dynamic that drives systems development in libraries must be the business aims of of the library service and the needs of its users, not the pace of technological change or the commercial motives of system suppliers to sell systems. It is not always necessary to be at the cutting edge of technology all of the time. It is not always possible to conduct a perfect selection process. Beyond a certain point, the law of diminishing returns will apply, whereby time and resources invested will provide only minimal benefits. In times of scarce resources in all sectors, library managers need to balance the need for investment in IT against the needs of other business areas and prioritize accordingly.

Skills for an open systems environment

System suppliers have moved from closed, proprietary systems to industry-standard systems, often 'jigsaw' systems using third-party components and middleware. System suppliers are increasingly looking to find new sources of income by diversifying into other value-added services such as facilities management, consultancy services and training. The context for these changes is a turbulent one. There is increasing competition and restructuring within the library systems industry, and there is evidence that system suppliers rather than cooperating more, are becoming more and more proprietary about their products. In this climate, system migration has become a very sensitive issue. Suppliers are generally unwilling to release information on product switching. 'Upgrading installed systems is a key competitive activity not only as a source of revenue but also as a means of securing existing customers and denying competitors market share.'[14]

It was once suggested that the library systems marketplace is 'an unholy alliance of compliant clients and complacent suppliers'. That statement, if it was ever true, is now well and truly a thing of the past. After the paradigm shift from manual to automated systems and the 'complacency' that followed, it could be argued that there is paradigm confusion in terms of both the library systems industry and the services it offers. These trends make it of paramount importance that library system managers preparing to migrate their system have an up-to-date understanding of current developments in computer systems at both technical and strategic levels, and that they keep abreast of market trends and company performance both within and beyond the library systems industry. It is no longer necessary for a library service to lock itself into one supplier for all its hardware and software requirements. Open systems based on industry-wide standards in a highly competitive marketplace make it imperative that library managers at least consider adopting a multivendor policy where significant sums are being spent. A multivendor approach potentially brings savings. But it also requires in-house IT expertise and business acumen which need to be continually updated by keeping up with the literature and attending third-party training courses, vendor user group meetings, conferences and seminars. Again, library managers need to make informed decisions about how far to apply multivendorism and how much in-house IT expertise can be afforded based on costs, benefits and potential opportunities.[15]

The case studies presented in this book demonstrate that a great deal of progress has been made in implementing IT in libraries and information centres, managing IT-related change and building effective collaborative partnerships with system suppliers. It is hoped that these case histories will contribute further to this learning process by identifying some of the skills, training needs and practices which need to be reviewed continually to enable us to adapt to the ever-changing environment in which we operate.

References

1   Machovec, G. S., 'The technology of change: what's involved and how it is accomplished', in Pitkin, G. M. (ed.), *Library systems migration: changing automated systems in libraries and information centers*, Meckler, 1991, 30.
2   Briscoe, G., 'Migration: a natural growth process for libraries (part one of two)', *Trends in law library management and technology*, 6 (7), March 1995, 1.
3   Saunders, L. M. and Kwon, M. L., 'The management of change: minimizing the negative impact on staff and patrons', in Pitkin, G. M., op. cit., 84.
4   Ibid., 73.
5   Ibid., 69.
6   See Scott Cree, J., Chapter 5, p. 120 (this volume).
7   Black, K., *Project management for library and information service professionals*,

London, Aslib, 1996.

8 Perley, D. R., *Implementing open systems*, London, McGraw-Hill, 1995, 11.

9 Ibid.

10 Cortez, E. M. and Smorch, T., *Planning second generation automated library systems*, Greenwood, 1993, 14–16.

11 Ross, J., 'Selecting library systems: a structured approach to minimising costs and optimising decisions', in Barton, D. (ed.), *Making choices: the selection of library computer systems: proceedings of a seminar held at Stamford, Lincolnshire, 20th June 1996*, Capital Planning Information Ltd, 1996, 35 (author's italics).

12 Heseltine, R., 'Choosing in the dark: strategic issues in the selection of library automation systems', *ITs news*, **27**, April 1993, 17.

13 Quinlan, C. A., 'The paradox of change: from turnkey system to in-house design', in Pitkin, G. M., op. cit., 86.

14 Blunden-Ellis, J. and Graham, M. E., 'A UK market survey of library automation system vendors (1992–1993)', *Program*, **28** (2), April 1994, 112.

15 Perley, D. R., op. cit., 28–30.

1 Managing library systems migration: matching theory and practice – a case study at Edge Hill University College

Ruth Jenkinson, Chris Lowe and Jenny Rowley

Introduction

The migration from one library management system to another is a significant project which will affect both operations as conducted by library staff and the services available to, and accessed by, users. It is, therefore, important that the transition from one system to another is managed effectively and efficiently. This chapter examines a variety of information systems methodologies in the context of a case study based on a systems migration project at Edge Hill University College, with the objective of moving towards the identification of the features of a methodology to support systems migration.

Information systems methodologies have been developed to support the analysis and design processes associated with the creation of new information systems. These methodologies, which we will review in more detail later, are intended to support the stages necessary in the design and implementation of a system from a functional specification. Library managers concerned with the implementation of a library management system are generally concerned to acquire either a turnkey package of hardware and software, or the hardware and software as two separate components, and then to configure elements of the system to suit specific requirements. They are not concerned with the analysis and design of a system, and the subsequent programming to create a tailored system, but rather with

- the identification of functional requirements
- the choice of a system that most closely meets those functional requirements, and the negotiation with suppliers to arrive at an appropriate specification
- adjustment and implementation of systems.

For most libraries, implementation strategies that ensure continuation of public services are of particular concern. Rowley[1] sought to propose some features of a library systems methodology. Here we develop this methodology further in the context of library systems migration via a case study approach.

The chapter discusses the case study in the context of three themes that might seem appropriate

- hard systems methodologies
- strategies for the management of change

- strategic information systems planning.

Edge Hill University College Learning Resource Centre

Library Services at Edge Hill operate on both the Ormskirk and Woodlands In-Service and Conference Centre (Chorley) Campuses. The service areas have a full-time equivalent staffing contingent of 25, with many part-time staff and some term-time only posts. In addition, students are employed to assist with shelving and related work.

The largest centre of activity is the Learning Resource Centre (LRC) on the Ormskirk campus. The Centre opened in January 1994, and is a purpose-built 4500 m^2 building on three floors. There are 500 reader spaces and workstations, including bookable carrels for quiet study, some with disabled access. The building has the capacity to house up to 250,000 items, up to 6000 of which will be on part-day loan for fast access. There are four bookable group rooms, two with IT facilities. The LRC contains the main book and audiovisual stock, plus a large periodicals collection and the Education Resource Collection of child-level material.

IT provision within the LRC includes over 150 state-of-the-art fully net-worked PCs with access to CD-ROM, word-processing and spreadsheet pack-ages. Fifty of the workstations have multimedia facilities and 25 of those have satellite distribution through the PCs. Other audiovisual facilities include audio and video playback facilities. Specialist support for these services is pro-vided by staff from Computer Services and MediaTech Services.

The Woodland Library collection consists of approximately 25,000 items, including books, periodicals and child-level material, and it mainly supports in-service courses for teachers and other professionals. There are networked IT facilities with links to the main campus at Ormskirk.

Most of the library systems are fully automated, with access to the library OPAC from any PC linked to the network. The Woodlands campus library and MediaTech loans service also operate through the library system. Self-issue, online ordering and electronic document delivery are all planned.

Close relationships with students and staff of the five College Schools are maintained and developed through the Schools Liaison Service. Library Services staff attend School and Course Boards, work with teaching staff on the selection and acquisition of relevant learning material and offer workshops and specialist advice to students and staff on using the LRC and its services.

Hard information-systems methodologies

Before a new system is installed, a formal study will usually be undertaken to investigate its nature and potential. Changes in information systems are likely to affect work patterns and, sometimes, the nature of the public service offered by the library to its customers. Thus, careful management of any computeriza-tion programme is vital. An organized systems development project will con-tribute to a successful system implementation. An information-systems methodology offers such an approach.

An information-systems methodology is a methodical approach to information-systems planning, analysis and design. A methodology is a body of methods, rules and postulates employed by a discipline. It involves recommendations about phases, subphases and tasks:

- when to use which and their sequence
- what sort of people should perform each task
- what documents, products and reports should result from each phase
- management, control, evaluation and planning of developments.

Information-system methodologies have been developed by systems developers and designers as a tool to aid in modelling information systems and designing a computer-based system which meets the requirements of the user of the information. Information-systems methodologies have not been designed to assist the purchaser of a computer system to select a specific system, although there are good reasons why such a purchaser might borrow some of the tools and approaches of the recognized methodologies to assist in a systematic analysis of requirements and specification of a system. Certainly, where a large and complex system is being considered, the adoption of a clearly defined methodology may well lead to more effective systems.

The adoption of a systematic approach to information-systems development offers a number of advantages. Broadly, the advantages for the manager include

- control over planning, since progress can be charted and financial allocations predicted
- standardized documentation, which assists in communication throughout the systems planning and life
- continuity provided as a contingency against key members of staff leaving the systems staff.

Advantages to those responsible for the information systems include that

- consideration of the requirements of any computer-based system requires the collection of many items of data and a systematic approach helps to ensure completeness and facilitate collation
- having to produce details formally in writing encourages more careful consideration of each issue, which is more likely to lead to well-founded recommendations and conclusions.

Although hard systems development methodologies vary, the following five main stages are commonly featured:

- definition of objectives

- definition of systems requirements
- design
- implementation
- evaluation.

Figure 1.1 gives a more complete summary of some of the typical elements of such stages. Rowley[2] translates these stages into

- definition of objectives
- specification of requirements
- systems design
- systems implementation
- systems evaluation.

The systems migration was analysed in terms of these stages and the structured approach with specific stages was generally helpful, but it is noted that the definition of objectives and the specification of requirements phases merged into one another and that it is not always possible to work through the stages in order.

Edge Hill case study

Definition of objectives

Perhaps this phase is best viewed as the pre-planning phase. Certainly, in a systems migration project the objectives of the systems project emerge from the weaknesses of any existing system. For Edge Hill there were concerns regarding the future of the existing system. The challenges that emerged from experi-

Definition of objectives	Terms of reference developed; initial needs analysis as a study proposal, leads to feasibility study, including evaluation of options and analysis of existing systems.
Definition of systems requirements	Specification of systems requirements.
Design phase	Logical systems model; physical systems model; choice and ordering of hardware and software configuration.
Implementation phase	Planning and preparation; education and training; database creation; system installation; switch-over.
Evaluation phase	Initial evaluation, on-going monitoring, maintenance, evolution.

Fig.1.1 *Summary of stages in systems analysis and design*

ence with the existing system led to the identification of certain characteristics as being essential in any new system. Thus, experience of the existing system was central in framing some of the key features of the proposed system. Key features that were sought in the new system included the following:

- **Stability** Fundamentally, the existing system had been sold by its suppliers to a relatively large number of small sites, and was sold on various platforms and formats. Further, the suppliers had been willing to configure the system to suit individual applications. Edge Hill's system had had a number of such tailored functions. Problems had already been experienced when an earlier system upgrade had been adopted. The upgrade eliminated much of the work that had been conducted on the additional functions and much work had to be conducted in configuring the upgrade in order to retrieve the functionality of the Edge Hill pre-upgrade system. Such changes often provoked other problems elsewhere in the system, such that there was no confidence that making any changes to the system would not cause something else to go wrong. This experience was shared by a number of users and generally undermined confidence in the long-term future of the system.
- **Capacity** In addition, in Edge Hill's current system, both hardware and software components of the system were working to capacity. Increasingly, additional functions were sought that were not embedded in the original system. Hardware was close to capacity with current levels of activity. New sites still needed to be added if the system was to serve all of the College sites on which a library service was offered.
- **Academic library loans** The opportunity was sought to identify a system that allowed the parameters for the loans system to accommodate the vagaries of term-time and assorted loan statuses characteristic of an academic institution.
- **Customer focused interfaces** Edge Hill was alert to the need to provide a system with a customer interface that offered the information required by the user, rather than the information that the systems supplier or the library had available. Too many systems still had a provider-oriented rather than a customer-oriented interface.
- **MARC (machine-readable cataloguing) record format** The ability to handle catalogue records in the MARC record format was an important feature. This facilitated the use of external MARC records and, in addition, supported searching on format to identify items in a specific medium, such as video or CD-ROM.
- **Additional features** Self-renewal, self-reservation and self-issue were viewed as important additional facilities in the circulation control part of the system. Such facilities would free staff for other activities associated with the effective use of the library resources.

Definition of systems requirements

The planning phase of the project commenced with the drafting of the functional specification.

The system was defined in the functional specification, which was prepared by the systems librarian. In systems migration, the systems librarian was able to benefit from

- experience and feedback based on the present system, relating both to its weaknesses and successes
- future needs
- an experience of larger system, in other libraries.

In drafting the specification, particular attention was paid to facilities that were seen to be important in a college library context, such as financial control, circulation control and the user perspective. The services of a management consultant were engaged in order to develop a clear and specific checklist of the functions required in the area of financial control. In particular, the system needed to interface effectively with the College finance systems. Circulation control was the second priority, since it consumes significant staff time; it was important that circulation control functions could be completed quickly and efficiently. Finally, particularly during demonstrations, systems were evaluated from the customer's perspective. It was not feasible to involve users directly at this point in the planning process, but staff exploited their considerable expertise of user access to library resources in order to assess the features of the OPAC and self-issue within the circulation control module.

The functional specification related to the software alone. The College already had a contract with ICL under which it had acquired two minicomputers: one to support the library system and one to support HEMIS, the student records system. In order to enhance reliability and security, it was intended that mirroring would operate between these two machines. Despite the claims of many suppliers concerning open systems, hardware constrained the choice of system. Library systems are often treated separately from other systems and are, in reality, less open than they might appear. Six potential suppliers were identified and asked to tender. Three of these did not tender either because their software would not run on an ICL platform or because they were only interested in supplying a turnkey package comprising both hardware and software. The three other systems suppliers did tender.

Demonstrations during the Easter vacation were requested from those suppliers who tendered and two of these provided a two-day demonstration. The timing was now tight since there was pressure to acquire the system from the existing year's budget. Ultimately, there was a difference of several thousand pounds between one tender and the other two. The supplier that eventually won the contract offered a particularly favourable package because they were concerned to sign up a college, and a college that had a new building that could be used as a showcase for their system.

Implementation

Implementation or actual physical migration of systems in academic libraries needs to be phased with the academic year, and it was important that any major transitions took place over the summer vacation. The practical aspects of implementation are of particular interest in migration.

The decision was made to go live with the system at the Woodlands site of the College first, in April. The Woodlands site had not previously had any experience of automation and was still operating on the Browne issue system. This presented some interesting issues with respect to the management of change which we reflect upon in the next section. The implementation of a new system at Woodlands presented more of a challenge for the staff at that site than it would have done for staff working at the central site which moved to an automated system over ten years ago. In addition to the benefits associated with change management at Woodlands, Woodlands is a small site on which it would be relatively easy to test the system. So this allowed pilot operation with parallel running of the old system at the central site in Ormskirk.

Parallel running was a significant feature of the changeover on the main site. Changeover was chosen for the summer period. In April, all bibliographic records were ported to the new system. Final-year student records did not need to be transferred to the new system. All loans were entered into the new system from 20 June, whilst returns were still being entered on the old system. On 10 July, 3000 transactions were manually transferred from the old system to the new system. Thus, during the period from Easter to June two sets of files were in operation. Some nine months after the beginning of the transfer, some of the ordering system was still running on the old system and did so until the end of the financial year.

Training is also an important part of the changeover process. As an integral part of the package, 12–16 days of training were available – some at the supplier's site and some at Ormskirk. A careful training schedule was devised, taking into account who needed to know what and who could train which other staff. In addition to formal training, it was also important to recognize that staff needed practice time and to build such time into the training schedules. The experience of training the Woodlands staff helped in refining this schedule. User training on the OPACs was offered for staff and students. This was also a vehicle for consultation with users with respect to the front end. Some amendments were made as a result of these sessions and this helped users to take ownership of the new system and to feel more satisfied that it met their needs.

Evaluation

Evaluation and development are and must be on-going. Two important aspects of evaluation and development deserve further comment.

User evaluation is performed through a suggestions scheme. Reassuringly often, suggestions received from users relate to issues that the systems librarian has already raised with the supplier. Nevertheless, user evaluation, although important, is only part of the picture, since only about one-third of the system is visible to the user, whilst two-thirds is used only by library staff.

The library has welcomed the uniformity of the new system across all of its user sites. The supplier has sought and been awarded ISO 9000, and this ensures that all procedures are well documented. There is an opportunity through the user group to contribute to the prioritization of development features in the next release.

Managing change

The literature on the management of change recognizes that change will only be successful if people as well as systems change.[3] Change will happen when the forces for change are stronger than the resisting forces. In order for people to make a positive contribution in a change situation, the manager must adopt an appropriate change strategy. Possible change strategies are

- directive, where the manager makes a decision and indicates the direction in which he or she expects change to take place
- normative, where the manager seeks to win the 'hearts and minds' of staff and to persuade them to share his or her vision of the positive value of change
- negotiating, where bargaining in the form of 'if you do this, I will do that' is employed
- action centred, where change is tried, experimented with and introduced on a step-by-step basis without necessarily defining the ultimate outcome in advance
- analytical, where the best changes are identified by an expert, for example a consultant, and his or her advice is taken in selecting the changes.

These strategies have not been discussed extensively in the context of information systems, despite the fact that information systems either within the organization or outside it have been responsible for much of the recent change in organizational structure, culture and marketplace. This may be because with information-systems implementation it is always possible to resort to taking away people's old systems and presenting them with new systems so that they have no option but to use the new system. In this context, it is relatively easy to adopt a focus on the directive and analytical strategies. However, without some application of normative and negotiating strategies there is not much chance that the user will use the system effectively and enjoy the experience.

Edge Hill case study

The most interesting part of the migration from the management of change perspective is the introduction of the new system at the Woodlands site. The Woodlands site is staffed by three part-time library assistants who have been isolated from the automation that was well established in other parts of the library. In addition, they had a demanding deputy and head teacher client group, some of whom were also unfamiliar with computer-based library systems. The opportunity for staff at Woodlands to be at the forefront rather than in their usual place in the rearguard of developments was taken.

Initially, staff at Woodlands were concerned both about the introduction of a computer-based system and about going live before the main site. However, the staff had no choice in the system or in the strategy for the changeover – the change strategy at this stage was distinctly directive. Furthermore, it was important that the system work effectively from day one, so there was no scope for error. Nevertheless, it was important that staff saw the changeover as a challenge and an opportunity and not as a threat. This was achieved partly through facilitating the changeover and lending generous support so that operational problems were minimized, and thereby, winning over staff to the new system. So, for example, additional staffing resources were allocated to Woodlands to support the entry of the data from the card catalogue into the new system, so that 80% of the stock was in the system before the system went live. Training was also important in creating confidence. Support was particularly important because as the system was introduced, it became evident that there were still inconsistencies between practices on the Woodlands site and those at the Ormskirk site. Thus, as part of the implementation, it was necessary to conduct some streamlining of processes across sites.

Strategic information-systems planning

The earlier sections in this chapter have described the case study from a perspective that might be considered as the traditional approach to systems analysis and design. This offers a useful perspective at the individual project level. In recent years, there has been a growing awareness that information-systems planning within organizations should be integral to the organization's strategic plan. This has led to developments in the approach to the management of information systems. This approach can be described as strategic information-systems planning (SISP). SISP is the process of establishing a programme for the implementation and use of information systems in such a way that it will optimize the effectiveness of the organization's information resources and use them to support the objectives of the whole enterprise as much as possible. The outcomes of an SISP are typically a short-term plan for the next 12–18 months, as well as a longer-term plan for the next 3–5 years. SISP has been evolving over the last ten years, fuelled by the recognition that the hardware/software approach to information-systems planning was not producing results either for the information systems department or for the organization as a whole. Put very simply, it has become clear that information systems are so integral to effective management, that managers at all levels, including the very top, need to participate in information-systems planning.

SISP has yet to be widely applied in library contexts, although the major information departments in proactive organizations should be participating in such a process. In considering the application of SISP to academic and public libraries, it is necessary first to define the organization, then to identify its strategic objectives and strategic planning process. The organization may be regarded as the library itself or the wider organization that the library serves. It is relatively straightforward to look at the wider objectives of an academic institution and to consider the contribution of the library and its systems towards the achievement of those objectives. Public libraries have a rather less well defined wider organizational context in which to operate and may prefer to restrict their consideration of organizational planning to the library itself. In principle, it is clearly wise that information-systems planning should be integral to the planning process for the wider organization.

The central focus of SISP is the matching of computer applications with the objectives of the organization in order to maximize the return on investment in information systems. SISP has a dual nature. It covers both detailed planning and budgeting for information systems at one level, and strategic issues and formulation at another. One of the characteristics of SISP is that in some cases it leads management to reassess the appropriateness of the enterprise's objectives and strategies, and it has occasionally been known to lead to major strategic reformulation.

SISP is a complex planning activity which requires a small project team, supported by input from a relatively large number of members of staff and possibly consultants. SISP is usually conducted as a project lasting for three to six months. It is important that the scope of the project is defined at the outset. The scope may be the whole organization or, more narrowly, just a department. SISP is appropriate for organizations which are already mature users of IT and treat information systems as a central support facility.

Figure 1.2 lists 20 steps that might lead to the creation of an SISP. These steps can be grouped into the following seven phases:

- Steps 1–3 are associated with setting the development of SISP into action.
- Steps 4–8 are concerned with identifying and formulating goals, objectives, missions and strategies for the organization. The process involves the identification of critical success factors or key factors for organizational success.
- Steps 9–11 consider the existing information systems through a systems audit.
- Steps 12–14 identify as many information-systems opportunities as possible, with a focus on the way in which systems can be used to achieve competitive advantage. These opportunities are filtered in order to identify those which offer the best return on investment.
- Step 15 leads to the production of an action plan.
- Steps 16–18 are concerned with the implementation and adoption of the action plan.
- Steps 19–20 focus on maintenance of the SISP.

1 Obtain authorization.
2 Establish a team and arrange accommodation, tolls, etc.
3 Allocate responsibilities and create a timetable.
4 Determine the corporate goals, objectives, missions, etc.
5 Establish the firm's corporate strategy, explicitly or implicitly.
6 Define the critical success factors.
7 Establish the key performance indictors.
8 Define the critical data set.
9 Incorporate the firm's information technology architecture.
10 Conduct a systems audit.
11 Rank current systems condition and prioritize current systems proposals.
12 Brainstorm for new systems and create an IT opportunities list.
13 Perform cost benefit at risk analysis.
14 Conduct filtering workshops.
15 Produce an action plan.
16 Communicate the action plan to all appropriate staff.
17 Identify and appear project champions.
18 Arrange for top management to commit publicly to SISP.
19 Create feedback mechanisms.
20 Update the SISP.

Fig.1.2 *Twenty steps to an SISP*

Methodologies for planning are now emerging. Methodologies must incorporate some or all of the elements of strategic planning, and must identify broad-based goals for information systems as well as the key means of achieving them. There are a number of different methodologies available and all of the major consultancy companies have proprietary approaches to SISP.

Edge Hill case study

Edge Hill has not adopted an SISP methodology for the strategic development of its information systems on a College-wide basis, although subsequent to the project described in this chapter it has developed a strategic planning process that includes contributions from service areas including information systems. Accordingly, the detailed stages of SISP as summarized in Figure 1.2 do not have much relevance in the context of this case study, but there are some aspects of the strategic approach that will be worthwhile to present.

Is the replacement of a library management system a strategic issue for the College?

Is the replacement of a library management system likely to have an impact on the competitive position of the College? In the sense that access to an appropriate range of library resources is central to learning and one of the key customer services offered to students, the answer has to be in the affirmative. Yet, there is a sense in which the replacement of the library management system was not perceived to be a strategic issue. For example, the upgrade of the student record system, HEMIS, was perceived as 'more' strategic, because the impact across a number of departments was more evident. The library management system was seen as directly owned by one department, the LRC, and therefore was not owned at a corporate level to the same extent. This attitude had implications for the embedding of the proposed development in the strategic planning process.

Strategic planning process

The acquisition of a new library management system involves considerable expenditure, which requires identification in strategic plans and in the budget process. Until relatively recently, strategic plans in higher education institutions were documents that were designed to communicate to the Funding Council the way in which the higher education institution planned to use any resources that the Funding Council might make available. The plan was therefore often created by top management with little consultation, and the interface between any functional strategy documents and the organization documents was not always as well managed as it might have been. Similarly, the link between financial planning and strategic planning processes was more tenuous that it should have been. Accordingly, the initiative to change was in the 1993–4 LRC operating objectives which was one year before it appeared in the 1994–5 College operating objectives.

Critical success factors

A key feature of an SISP is the identification of critical success factors. Without these, it might be argued that a strategic approach to information-systems planning can be described as planning, but not strategic. The wider application of SISP in many functional areas within organizations, and specifically libraries, awaits an agreement concerning the definition of critical success factors.

Who defines the critical success factors? – the library manager, top management, tutors or students? There are many problems with all of these groups in defining critical success factors. It is reasonable to look for some customer focus in the definition of critical success factors. Interaction with students suggests that their definition of a good library service is a library that can deliver books and information when they are required. What other success factors characterize a quality library service?

Continuing the story – the Edge Hill case study

Information systems development is a continuous cycle, as shown in the systems lifecycle in Figure 1.3. This chapter has focused primarily on a specific migration project, when the library transferred from one system to another. In general, this was a very successful transition and the system has now been operational for well over a year. This brief coda to the case study is included to reflect the continuing issues associated with system development. During summer 1996, an attempt was made to install an upgrade of the system software. The system was shut down for one week during August 1996 with a view to installing the software upgrade. This upgrade installation was unsuccessful, and the library had to revert to the old system, pending a further attempt to install the upgrade planned for Christmas 1996. The project was aborted due to significant difficulties in transferring the database into the new system.

Sometimes more lessons are to be learnt from failure than success. We, therefore, share these lessons and our enhanced appreciation of the wider issues associated with software upgrades. The key dynamic that needed more careful management and controlled intervention was associated with the fact that the Geac system was installed on an ICL UNIX file server, running under UNIVERS. Staff at ICL were responsible for supporting the file server and UNIX; Computer Services staff at Edge Hill had responsibility for local applications and databases; and Geac were responsible for the library system. Essentially, the library was acting as the customer for the three different agencies. This situation was aggravated by these agencies' lack of experience in working together on this type of configuration. The LRC manager needed to act as intermediary between these agencies in order to facilitate the process. Specific lessons were

- book internal computer services support and do not assume that it will be available
- resolve any technical problems with tests and pilot runs prior to the main changeover

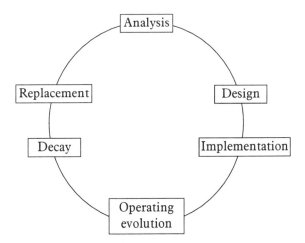

Fig.1.3 *The systems lifecycle*

- make many back-up copies of the database (the normal convention is to make three copies, however, seven copies would allow much more leeway for failed attempts to convert the database which result in corrupted data)
- be aware of the library systems supplier's experience of installing upgrades on your specific platform.

Conclusions

This chapter has explored the migration from one library management system to another. It introduces some features of information-systems methodologies and then applies them to a case study at Edge Hill University College. The main systems migration project was successful, although a subsequent software upgrade project presented its own problems. Finally, systems migration is a learning experience in the management change that embraces both systems and people.

References

1 Rowley, J. E., 'Aspects of a library systems methodology', *Journal of information science*, **20** (1), 1994, 41–6.
2 Ibid.
3 See, for example, Lewin, K., *Field theory in social science*, Harper, 1951.

Further reading

Avison, D. E. and Fitzgerald, G., *Information systems development: methodologies, techniques and tools*, Oxford, Blackwell, 1988.

Checkland, P., *Systems thinking, systems practice*, Chichester, Wiley, 1991.

Clayton, M. and Batt, C., *Managing library automation*, 2nd edn, Aldershot, Gower, 1992.

Cutts, G., *Structured systems analysis and design methodology*, 2nd edn, Oxford, Blackwell, 1991.

Daniels, A. and Yeates, D., *Basic systems analysis*, 2nd edn, London, Pitman, 1984.

Downs, E. et al., *Structured systems analysis and design method: application and content*, London, Prentice-Hall, 1988.

Mason, D. and Willcocks, L., *Systems analysis, systems design*, Henley-on-Thames, Alfred Waller, 1994.

National Computing Centre, *Systems training library*, 2nd edn, Oxford, Blackwells, 1990.

Ole, T. W. et al., *Information systems methodologies: a framework for understanding*, Wokingham, Addison-Wesley, 1988.

Remenyi, D. S. J., *Introducing strategic information systems planning*, Oxford, NCC/Blackwell, 1991.

Rowley, J. E., 'Strategic information systems planning', *Information services and use*, **15** (1), 1995, 57–66.

Ward, J. et al., *Strategic planning for information systems*, Chichester, Wiley, 1990.

2 From proprietary to open systems in Suffolk Libraries & Heritage

Guenever Pachent and Douglas Reed

Introduction

Suffolk is the easternmost county in Britain, with a diversity of landscape from the North Sea coast in the east to the heaths of Newmarket in the west, and from the forests of Breckland and the Suffolk Broads in the north to the pastures of the Stour valley and Constable country in the south.

Suffolk has a population of 657,000, with a density of only 1.7 per hectare, compared with 2.4 per hectare for Great Britain as a whole – a reflection of Suffolk's rural nature. Suffolk is a county of remote villages and ancient market towns, some of which, during the late nineteenth century, became pockets of industrialization and urbanization. As these nineteenth century industries declined, service industries and commercial activities superseded them and today the most important centres are on the River Orwell, namely the county town of Ipswich, the largest in Suffolk with a population of around 116,000, and the container port of Felixstowe, which is the largest in the UK and the fourth largest in Europe. Although the economic base of the county is healthy and diverse, with agriculture and tourism major contributors, the fishing port of Lowestoft has suffered from the decline in the fishing industry and unemployment in the town is over 9%.

The population varies from affluent to poor, and in familiarity with information systems from the IT literate workers in BT's research centre at Martlesham to those who have never used a computer.

While communications from Newmarket in the west to Ipswich and Felixstowe in the east are good, Lowestoft feels somewhat isolated in the north, the villages in the centre of the county are served by the inadequate Ipswich to Norwich road, and across the county the villages and hamlets are linked by winding lanes, occupied during the harvest and sugar beet seasons by slow-moving farm vehicles.

Suffolk County Council has a statutory duty to provide a comprehensive library service in Suffolk and to preserve the official archives. It also delivers a comprehensive archive service.

Libraries & Heritage is a department and a committee of the County Council. It encompasses libraries, archives, arts and museums and its objectives cover the provision of information, the delivery of leisure services, the support of education and the preservation and exploitation of heritage and culture.

Libraries & Heritage provides services to the people of Suffolk through 41 branch libraries, eight mobile libraries, three school library service centres, three mobile libraries for schools, one hospital and three prison libraries, and three record offices. Housebound users choose their books in their own homes through the Home Library Service. Only three of the static libraries have a catchment population of more than 40,000, whereas 13 serve areas with populations of less than 4000.

People can choose from over a million books and some 60,000 audio and video items. All 41 static libraries are online and customers may choose to borrow, return, renew, reserve and collect items at any branch. Each year, over six million books and around 300,000 other materials are issued, nearly one million enquiries answered, and around 195,000 reservations supplied. Regular stock exchanges amount to 330,000 books changing location each year and these, with the 158,000 new acquisitions added, ensure a changing selection of materials at each library. During the year, 4.8 million visits are made by Suffolk people to the county's libraries and 52% of the population hold current library cards.

Libraries & Heritage provides the archive service through three record offices which contain 1123 m^3 of records – an extensive collection of material dating from the twelfth century relating to Suffolk's diverse and significant history. The archive service is twice as busy as any other UK county archive service, receiving 43,000 visits a year, not only from Suffolk residents but also from people from all over the world.

Suffolk's first generation library system was a Plessey batch processed solution. The second generation system was an online Geac 9000 and the third generation system is DS Ltd's Galaxy 2000. The record offices have been automated for the first time in 1996, apart from an earlier pilot of the MDA's MODES data entry system, using DS Ltd's CALM 2000.

The size of the Suffolk library information system is shown by the statistics in Figure 2.1. Figures 2.2 and 2.3 show the extent of the impact of automation.

This chapter will inevitably show DS Ltd's third generation system Galaxy 2000 as an improvement on Geac's second generation 9000 system. It is important to us that readers understand that we are not comparing the companies but two generations of system. Just as DS supplies Galaxy 2000, Geac markets an elegant and multifunctional third generation system. Just as Geac supplied a second generation system in the 9000, DS provided a second generation system called Galaxy. Galaxy 2000 was the third generation product which best met our needs in late 1994 and our decision in no way suggests that Geac does not have on the market an excellent third generation product.

Hardware
- main server – Sun Sparcserver 1000E
  2 x 60MHz processors
  18 GB disk storage: mirrored
  896MB RAM
  5 GB + 20 GB tape stacker
- 215 staff terminals
- 123 public terminals
- all terminals are PCs

Application software
- acquisitions
  1031 orders weekly average
  2900 books receipted weekly average
  240 sound and vision items weekly average
  29,480 catalogue records added 1995–6 (less than a full year)
  all stock receipted centrally
  prepublication data loaded weekly – average 300 bibliographic records
- catalogue
  database of 428,410 bibliographic records
  3,287,500 MARC tag records
  1.2 million item records – 158,000 additions each year
  access paths include ISBN, author, title, keyword and relevance ranked
       phrases, class mark, publisher and combinations of these
  fast, easy access to accurate bibliographic data for staff and public
- circulation
  database of 400,000 borrower records
  up to 20 related item records
  up to 20 related reservation records
  no limit on account records
  process up to 15,000 transactions per hour with a 2-second response
       time
  200 + reservations on popular fiction titles by publication date

Fig. 2.1 *Size of Galaxy 2000 in Suffolk*

General software
- operating system Solaris 2.4
- RDBMS Ingres 6.4
- staff terminals run extended VT220
- viewpoint – Windows based – Visual Basic
- TCP/IP via LAN Workplace for DOS
- LAN printing via Personal Netware

Application software
- circulation with cash management, ILL and automated stock exchange under development
- catalogue including local studies
- Z39.50 (server and client) under development
- community information
- acquisitions
- messaging
- management information
- networked access to JMLS' LIBTEL II, WWW, newspapers on CD-ROM
- OPAC with clear navigational aids
- Web catalogue and dial-in
- self-service reservation
- self-service renewal
- self-service electronic comments
- self-service issue (under development)
- e-mail/office applications due over routed network 1997

Networking
- all 45 buildings online (12 kilostream, 66 ISDN lines)
- TCP/IP and IPX (the latter to be phased out – not permitted on corporate routed network)
- all service points have routers
- all service points have Class C subnet addresses
- structured cabling – UTP Category 5
- part of corporate routed network

Fig. 2.2 *Galaxy 2000 applications in Suffolk*

Hardware
- 3 local servers – Intel 486SX PCs
  25MHz processors
  420 MB disk storage
  8 MB RAM
  back-up across network to central Sun Sparcserver
- 15 staff terminals
- 17 public terminals
- all terminals are PCs

Application software
- full 32-bit application
- full-text retrieval – Dscribe (based on Idealist)
- full graphical user interface
- accessions
- catalogue
- conservation
- records management

Fig.2.3 *CALM 2000 in Suffolk*

Automation history

There is a view that IT and networking are acceptable for central and urban libraries but too expensive to install in rural libraries. In fact the opposite is true. IT is the only cost-effective way of providing some services in remote rural libraries and it is an essential tool in rural library provision.

Suffolk has taken this view since the 1970s. From the first microfiche catalogue and batch processed issue system, all 41 branch libraries were part of the Suffolk IT network. No branch library, even those open for ten hours a week in shared community premises, was hived off from the mainstream IT development.

This was a defining decision for Suffolk and one that has never been regretted: the point at which Suffolk library service recognized the potential of automation and became in principle one library with 41 access points. This decision shaped the second and third generation systems which put the principle into practice.

First generation (batch issue) system

Suffolk County Council had been created in 1974 from five predecessor county and borough councils. The legacy for the Suffolk county library service was a variety of manual issue systems and card catalogues of varying quality, accuracy and coverage.

From the late 1970s, new books were catalogued onto the Suffolk microfiche catalogue using British Library MARC records. The work was carried out by the authority's computer unit.

In 1980, Suffolk started installing a Plessey batch processed issue system. The ten or so larger libraries were connected by BT lines to area processing units in the central libraries while the remainder collected their issue data on cassettes in portable data capture units. The cassettes were sent to the centre using the van delivery service. All the batched data (issues, renewals, returns, additions, deletions and stock exchanges) was processed by the Computer Unit which also printed the overdue notices.

It is difficult now to recall the benefits of that batch system, while the negative features spring readily to mind. The batch system brought machinery into libraries without the benefits of online services. It regularly produced false overdue notices: staff would realize that the week's notices had been posted when borrowers came in with their overdue postcards and insisted, generally correctly, that they had already returned the items concerned. The system could not tell users which books they had out on loan, irritating the borrowers who recalled that, within parameters, even the Browne issue system could do that. The new light pens did not always read the barcodes and users saw the automated system taking longer and producing fewer benefits than the manual system.

However, there were major benefits to the batch system which both improved service and efficiency at the time and provided the foundations for the online systems which were to follow.

The foundations for the future were the computerized county-wide electronic catalogue (produced then in batch mode on microfiche but later loaded into the second generation online system), the barcoding of every book with a link to the appropriate catalogue record, and the electronic borrower database and the issue of barcoded library cards to all 350,000 borrowers.

The service benefit of the batch system was the creation and maintenance of the county-wide microfiche catalogue and its consequent improvement to reservation supply times. The fiche catalogue was amended with additions and deletions and, equally importantly in a rural library system, with stock exchange locations. It could be as much as three months out of date, and year-by-year it suffered from an increasing number of inaccuracies, but it still enabled reservations to be sent direct to a library and for the book to be 'trapped' on return. This was a remarkable improvement on the previous situation when it had taken up to six weeks to establish whether or not Suffolk had a copy of a given title.

The efficiency benefits of the batch system related to the automated issue, renewal and discharge, the automated production of the catalogue, and the automated printing of overdue notices. It was at this stage of automation that efficiency savings were made. In Suffolk terms, this meant the non-recruitment of staff who would have been necessary to maintain manual systems in the face of rising library usage. The efficiencies brought about by the two later online systems were outweighed by the service enhancements which demanded staff time. There was no opportunity for overall efficiency savings at these later stages, although work was reallocated.

As we watch our archive service automating for the first time using sophisticated text retrieval software and industry-standard communications, there is a touch of envy: if only the first generation library systems had been able to use this technology! However, it will take years to convert the archive catalogues and documents into electronic form and, thus, years for it to become a usable retrieval and production tool. The library system, because all data has been in electronic form for so long, does not have this problem and is a finished usable and user-friendly system today.

So what did we learn from the batch system? It left the indelible lesson that batch is not a solution. For this reason we will not support the automation of mobile libraries until there is a mobile communications system resilient enough to support an online system.

It has probably also led to the belief that the online system with which the batch system was replaced would bring only benefits, not problems. It did so in the end, but it took two or three years to reach that point. During that time the product remained damaged by our initial unrealized expectations as well as its own lack of resilience.

We also learnt that the corporate computer unit could not be relied on (at that time) to give a consistently high priority to library processing; departments with bigger budgets were given a higher priority than the library service. If problems occurred, batch data might not be processed on time and notices could be delayed. That experience led us to go it alone, when we chose the second generation system, with a departmental turnkey (a misnomer if ever there was one) information and library system.

Second generation information and library system

We chose our second generation system (a Geac 9000) in 1986 and installed it in 1987–8, over a 15-month period. Although the people involved most in its selection have since retired, it was selected, we believe, in preference to newer products such as CLSI, because the functionality was not only comprehensive but also tried and tested, if only on the Geac 8000. We contracted to buy 250 terminals for installation in 45 locations. Service points were connected by a mixture of kilostream and 9600 baud leased lines, using part X.25, part ANSI X3.28 Poll Select Protocol.

The size of the Suffolk enterprise required a Geac 9000 and the development of all the software for that machine. In the event, the 9000 was not finished in time for the Suffolk go live and we started instead on an 8000. We ran on an 8000 for about six months, an 8000 and 9000 combined for a few months, and then on the 9000 only.

This book is about lessons learnt from system implementations. Geac learnt that when Suffolk sets deadlines it means to keep to them, and we in Suffolk learnt that the sales representatives and managers of information and library system companies (the two that we know, anyway: Geac and DS Ltd) sometimes agree to deadlines which in the event their software analysts cannot meet.

The meeting of these two cultures led to an unhappy period distinguished in retrospect by a non-resilient system bedevilled by slow, sometimes unacceptably slow, response times. At one point, there were embarrassingly long queues at the issue desks and some staff were demoralized enough to threaten industrial action.

Only Geac can say what it learnt from the experience, but we learnt a great deal. This chapter will incorporate the lessons that are still relevant today.

Despite the initial misunderstandings, miscalculations and naïvetes, the Geac 9000 turned from caterpillar into butterfly. It delivered circulation, back-up, terminal emulation, acquisitions, OPAC, community information, e-mail and management information and also provided networked online connections to JMLS's LIBTEL II bibliographic database and to Essex's and Norfolk's Geac systems. It became resilient, in so far as a second generation system was able, and its response times, even on Saturday mornings and in half-term weeks, were excellent.

Its ability to satisfy internal reservations within a few days, even to village libraries in remote parts of the county, endeared it to library staff and users alike and it became a key issue in the debate as to whether Suffolk County Council should remain or be divided into four unitary authorities (in the event, the County Council was retained intact). Unlike the batch system, it produced reliable overdue notices and staff and customers came to trust it.

Systems management skills

The library and information management systems are marketed as turnkey systems which can be operated by library staff with minimal technical skills. We found that even the management of the second generation system which only provided library functionality (not much additional networked information, as is the case with the third generation system) was better managed by a systems manager with software and networking skills. We found that Geac expected our systems manager to have professional expertise and skills, and we were sometimes blamed for problems that occurred because we did not initially employ these skills.

Instead of forcing responsibility onto the supplier of the turnkey system we decided to upgrade the post of systems manager and employ a manager with software and communications expertise. This has paid dividends not only in the day-to-day management of systems, but also in assessing the performance of the suppliers, in the specification and selection of the third generation system, and in representing Libraries & Heritage's case in the development of corporate communications and the routed network.

Interestingly, the third generation system, and the growing but unrelated requirement for additional pieces of client software and PC support, has revealed a further training need among the 3.5 system centre staff. It has meant that the assistant systems managers have required training in Sun server administration, management information reports using SQL (structured query language), EDI (electronic data interchange), the Internet and Netscape, CD server administration, PC support and image management, as well as in the functionality of the library and record office applications. The skills requirement of library system centre staff is growing and is something that organizations must take account of and prepare for.

Leading or bleeding edge

The development of successful new generation library and information systems depends probably on the existence of risk-taking library services as well as risk-taking and innovative suppliers. In the development of IT, as in the development of the new book supply market or any significant change to the way libraries will operate in the future, there are leaders and followers. The leaders risk that the leading edge is in the event the bleeding edge and that the expected benefits of change are outweighed by the associated disruptions to service. The followers risk that there will be no leaders (and, thus, no development), that developments will not necessarily suit their service vision and that a late investment in change will not bring as high a rate of return. By this last point we mean that an IT installation has a finite life not only in the obvious area of hardware and software but also conceptually in its position in community and global networking. The earlier a library service can exploit a new opportunity through investment, the more cost-effective it will be.

Suffolk has been a leader in the development of both its second and third generation library and information systems, not out of any desire to lead the way but because its vision (an online service reaching a large number of service points over a wide and rural area, incorporating all transactions – including self-service – and consequently requiring fast response times) was groundbreaking. The Geac 9000 was tried and tested partly in Somerset but most critically on the large numbers of transactions in Suffolk, Lancashire and finally Essex. The results of everybody's efforts, not least those of Geac's tireless systems analysts, was a fast, efficient, high transaction, multifunctional library and information system which is still in 1996 doing the business in Essex (although it is due to be replaced soon, we understand, by Geac's third generation system).

Galaxy 2000 owes much to the courage of Birmingham for its initial investment in a concept much of which must have been 'vapourware' at the time, to Suffolk and Aston University for the specification and rapid installation of comprehensive functionality, including self-service, and of course to DS Ltd for its elegance and imagination. Suffolk also played a key part in testing the use of ISDN (integrated service digital network) for transaction processing.

CALM 2000 for Archives, DS's and Suffolk's first-cum-third generation system for archives, owes its development to investment by Suffolk in what was no more than a prototype and to the professional archivists of Hampshire and Suffolk for its ability to handle archival concepts.

Lessons from the bleeding edge

There are lessons to be learnt from the installation of untried systems. It is important to adhere to the customer service maxim 'underpromise and overdeliver', that is to underplay the strengths of the new system so that people are surprised and pleased by its features rather than disappointed by its failure to live up to expectations. This is the right approach to system implementation whether or not it is an untried system, but it is especially important if there are likely to be unforeseen problems.

It is necessary to acquire the support of staff and users so that they have a stake in the success of the project. They should, if possible, feel that they own the project, not that it has been thrust upon them. The steps we took to achieve this are described under 'Human issues' later.

When evaluating the system, it is important to learn as much as possible from reference site visits to existing customers. If it is new software, it may not be possible to see it in a working environment but it is possible to learn about the company: its strengths and weaknesses and how these might be expected to affect a new product.

We would also recommend the testing of software on site. In October 1995, we tested on-site in Suffolk, side-by-side, the software of the three shortlisted suppliers. We kept the software for two weeks and tested it in detail. This was a revealing exercise and played a significant part in our selection of the replacement system.

The interruptions to service experienced during the early days of the Geac 9000 taught us to put a high priority on resilience, back-up systems and support. The Galaxy 2000 application was developed under Ingres, which is a robust and resilient environment, itself designed for developing online transaction processing systems. Galaxy 2000 has full disk mirroring so that drives can fail and be replaced without disruption to service. The leased lines on the network are backed up by ISDN and, if there is a break in the communications network, traffic can be diverted along an alternative route. Issue, renewal, return and borrower registration can take place offline but this is seldom necessary – the few breaks to service which occur are usually caused by ISDN faults (requiring repair by BT) to single ISDN-only branches.

Having underestimated the use of the Geac 9000, we were very careful to provide our new supplier with accurate estimates of use. Not only did we have much improved information (because the Geac 9000 recorded our online levels of use), but also sizing is not quite as critical an issue today when processing power and disk space are relatively cheap.

Response times are absolutely critical on a transaction-processing network and our specification and contract are specific about our requirements. A contract covering all eventualities is essential but will be of little help if the supplier is trying its best to rectify a problematic situation. We think of the contract as the framework of the partnership, not a weapon to be invoked.

Finally, skills are needed to assess the proposals put forward by prospective suppliers so that potential problem areas can be identified and penetrating questions asked.

Selection of a new third generation system

Reasons for the change

As officers we took the decision in July 1993 not to upgrade the Geac 9000 any further but to start the process of replacement. There were three factors which forced this decision. First, the Geac acquisitions software had always been relatively inflexible and staff-intensive in a public library environment. We wanted to increase efficiency by passing electronic order messages both internally and externally using EDI. Although external EDI would have been possible, development of the electronic order environment internally was not feasible within the constraints of the second generation system. This was the defining moment when we realized that the second generation system could not deliver our ambitions for the future.

Second, we had provisionally agreed to install in August 1993 a major new release of circulation. This would have required all staff (some 500 in total) to receive half-a-day's training. We put the cost of this into the context of the training cost of a replacement system and decided to postpone the new release and thus the retraining of staff in circulation until there was a replacement system.

The third factor was Local Government Review. At the time, it was possible that Suffolk might be divided into four unitary authorities in 1996 or 1997. It was important to protect the county library service by bequeathing to any unitaries a modern, industry-standard library system which would be flexible enough to communicate with the IT systems of the new parent authorities. In this scenario, the new unitaries would be most likely to retain the county-wide IT system and the county-wide services which go with it. We estimated that the replacement system had to be installed in 1995 to meet this objective, and that specification, evaluation and selection therefore had to take place in 1994. We set the details of this timetable in November 1993 (see Figure 2.4) and we are proud that we kept to this timetable, taking the replacement system live in May and June 1995.

These three factors and the consequent timetable meant that Suffolk would again be near the leading edge of system implementation, because the third generation systems were very new. Some might say that we had not learnt the lessons of 1987 and 1988 – of the disruption that had then been caused by ground-breaking technology and could be repeated in 1995. We would say that we had learnt the important lessons described earlier and that we used understanding to minimize the risks in 1995, although the key risk remained the same: that the system we chose had not been proved to work at the level of transaction processing demanded by Suffolk use levels. In the event, and with

1993	
December	consult staff, December to May
	write specification
1994	
January	
February	
March	initial advert in *European journal*, mid-March
April	receive interest from suppliers by end of April
May	choose shortlist during May and complete specification, end of May
June	interim report to Libraries & Heritage Committee, June
July	shortlisted companies compile tenders, June to August
August	consult users, councillors, staff, June to August
September	evaluate tenders, negotiate, decide, September to November and interim report to Committee, September
October	further consultations with staff, members, users, September to November
November	final report to Committee, November
December	sign contract, December
1995	
January	prepare software for Suffolk, setting parameters, policies and priorities, January to March
February	
March	train staff, January to March
April	install between 17/4/95 and 30/6/95 (i.e. during libraries'
May	quietest period)
June	progress report to Committee, June

Fig. 2.4 *Original timetable for replacing library and information system*

only one significant hiccough with response times, Galaxy 2000 achieved its contracted swift response times.

Systems market

It is interesting to note that the players in the third generation library and information system market are nearly all the established companies who understand the complexities of library functions and have learnt how to provide them on, alongside and integrated with industry-standard hardware, software and communications. Six out of the seven companies which tendered for Suffolk's third generation system in August 1994 are well-known to the UK library market and some of them to the world-wide market. The seventh company tendered in partnership with an established South African library and information system supplier. Even in this instance there was no attempt to write systems from scratch.

This situation still apparently prevails: the companies being shortlisted for tenders by other library services we know have been in this specialist market for many years.

From one perspective this is to libraries' advantage because the companies understand library and information needs. The personnel understand what they are contracting to do. This must mean fewer risks than a partnership with an inexperienced company.

However, the drawback is that these companies have a stereotypical view of the library market, namely that it is acceptable to promise and not to deliver (on time or even at all) and that under-investment is inevitable because library services cannot pay for the services they want. As librarians and library managers we need more companies to break free of these assumptions, because neither is necessarily true. Here in Suffolk we know of more library services wanting to pay for development than of authorities unable to fund IT installations. The library and information system is critical to library operation and development and thus inevitably brings funding with it. As a profession and key community service, we need the system suppliers to recognize that there are not only third generation systems but also third generation customers whose approach to IT has developed just as IT has done over two decades.

It is unclear whether the traditional market is able to make this leap of understanding or whether it will take a new player to achieve it. So if there is out there a risk-taking leading library service and a new ambitious system supplier, go for it – we should all be in your debt.

Approach to selection

An analysis of the selection process which led to the purchase of Galaxy 2000 and CALM 2000 is set out in detail elsewhere,[1] and this chapter will not repeat the detail in that publication.

The main features of the Network '95 procurement project were

- the requirement for a third generation system at a time when they were at the very early stages of development
- a generalized specification couched in terms of outcomes, not detailed functionality
- a requirement for an information network and for archive cataloguing functions as well as for the traditional library housekeeping system
- an evaluation process which included demonstrations in libraries by the systems suppliers to the public (covered later under 'Human issues') and the testing of software on site.

We took our definition of a third generation system as that described by Heseltine[2] in 1992, that is

- industry-standard hardware, i.e. using PCs and a server running the UNIX operating system
- industry-standard communications, e.g. TCP/IP, ethernet (IEEE 802.3)
- industry-standard UNIX-based relational database management systems (RDBMS).

Although at the time, insistence on a third generation system was more a matter of faith than complete understanding, we are now clear about some of the benefits. The use of industry-standard products means that much of our software, which does not carry out the library housekeeping functions, is not written by the library system supplier but purchased by the supplier from a third party. Consequently, developments can be delivered much more promptly and the supplier's software resource concentrates on the development of library-specific functionality.

By developing the functionality in an industry-standard RDBMS, the software analysts use a fourth generation language (4GL) which enables rapid software development. As a customer, it is clear to see that functionality is developed more swiftly than it was with the second generation library system.

Use of the Internet-compatible TCP/IP communications standard means that the Libraries & Heritage network has become an integrated part of the County Council's routed network. The extent of the benefits of this are only just coming to light. For example, it will allow us to have integrated e-mail and word-processing stretching from library staff in the smallest branch libraries through headquarters staff on to colleagues in other departments and on to chief librarians and library users on the external Internet. Routed access to information held in other departments' systems, e.g. bus timetables in Transport, school statistics in Education, offers exciting possibilities. (There is a downside to the routed network: the demanding security requirements required in order not to expose the corporate networks to hacking. However, in our view, the benefits of seamless communications are worth the extra care required.)

Finally, the use of industry-standard hardware offers economies of scale. A typical PC in headquarters carries Netscape to surf the World Wide Web and other packages of client software to access Galaxy 2000, the corporate office system and Internet mail. At server level there are the following three reasons to purchase an NT server:

- to network over a wide area the archive system CALM 2000
- to hold and network information from CD-ROMs
- to hold and network Microsoft Office.

The aim is to purchase not three but two servers, thus making economies of scale.

Requirements
We described our requirements at the tender stage in general terms, specifying

desired outcomes rather than the way functions should work. As we evaluated systems our requirements became more specific, so that the final contract provides in particular for that functionality which was not in the standard product at the time of purchase. In other words, we did not waste time describing in the contract what the software could be seen to do, but we did take care over specifying how it should be developed. When we specified what we wanted from our third generation system, we set out to separate our future needs from our experience of the Geac 9000 (i.e. not to fall into the trap of specifying an upgraded Geac 9000), because only by doing this would we be open to the ideas of all companies in the market and the opportunities presented by technological developments. Nevertheless, our experience of this second generation system had very much shaped our views for the future.

Self-service

In both library and archive services, Suffolk has been committed for many years to offering choice to users by offering self-service facilities. The Suffolk Record Office was one of the first local authority record offices to offer self-service access to microfilm and fiche services and, similarly, the libraries were among the first to provide self-service reservation.

The Geac 9000 experience taught us a lot about what users wanted from their library network. Immediately upon installation of the public terminals in 1987 use rose dramatically above the previous use of the microfiche catalogue, this despite the fact that at that time we only offered the catalogue and the user's borrower record. This contributed significantly to our problems at the time of installation because the system was not sized for this amount of public usage. We dealt with this by bidding for and gaining additional funding from the County Council for an extra processor.

Public use remained high throughout the life of the Geac system. However, increasingly, there was discontent with the public interface and an acceptable and sophisticated public interface became a high priority for the replacement system. A key problem with the old OPACs was that they displayed codes to the public rather than words. Users found it easy enough to discover bibliographic records, but were unable to interpret the location and status information of relevant items. Therefore, much use of the OPACs resulted in frustration and failure through inability to locate the books. Also, during the period 1987–94, users were becoming increasingly exposed to Windows-based software at school, at work and in the home. This resulted in a growing perception among users that the text-based OPAC service on dumb terminals was old-fashioned.

When users were consulted about what they wanted (see 'Human issues' below), it was clear that they had become demanding of their system. As Figure 2.5 shows, they wanted not only the traditional catalogue but also extended and informative bibliographic records, access to external databases including, even in September 1994, the Internet, and magnified screens. There were mixed but informed views about whether the interface should be keyboard-, mouse- or

---

Feedback from library users provided the following clear messages.

- Library users were keen to have a new computer system.
- Many of them were knowledgeable about our second generation system, and had constructive ideas for a new system.
- They wanted new services, not just a more attractive version of the existing public terminals.
- They wanted access to networked CD-ROMs, to remote databases, to images and even to self-service issue and the superhighway.
- A significant number wanted magnified screens.
- They wanted self-service printers and scanners which work.
- They wanted sufficient numbers of public terminals.
- There was no clear preference for screen interface: some users preferred a Windows layout with icons and use of a mouse, others preferred to use keyboards, others said they would rather use touch screens.

Fig. 2.5 *Feedback from users, September 1994*

touchscreen-driven and there was acceptance of and some enthusiasm for the concept of self-service issue.

The 9000 experience had also taught us interesting lessons about self-service reservations. The second generation system had not been sized sufficiently to allow county-wide or global reservations as a matter of course: staff only were allowed to place these, and then only if there were not copies at area level (the system recognized that Suffolk divides into three administrative areas). Thus the public could only use self-service reservation on books in their area. If the books were outside their area, as they often were, users had to ask staff to place the reservations. This was unsatisfactory for the public.

The old system had also shown the complexities of prioritizing reservations and the difficulties in ensuring that reservations were met in fair chronological order. Indeed, on the old system they often were not. It was not uncommon to have a waiting list on a title in one area, while the same title sat unused on a library shelf in another area.

This led us in 1995 to dispose of the concept of area reservations and move both staff and public to global, county-wide reservations. Now staff and public place global reservations and staff have no more ability than users to influence a position on a waiting list. To cope with the fact that Suffolk is geographically large and the books have to be physically transported to the pick-up location, the system has sophisticated rules to determine which copy is chosen to meet a reservation. The system looks first for a copy in the local branch, then for a copy in an open branch in the area, then for a copy in an open branch in the county. If there are no copies on the shelf in open branches, the shelf check is regenerated the next day for open branches. Meanwhile, if a copy is returned at any time during this process, this copy is supplied instead.

The new self-service terminals not only allow users to place these global reservations but also to see the status of the book as it moves between libraries and arrives on the reservation shelf.

When we moved users to the replacement self-service terminals in 1995, we found that we had underestimated their attachment to certain features of the old service. This is a tribute to the excellent functionality of the Geac 9000 public terminals. We went live without a Dewey search (although subject searching was available) or self-service reservations and the users were vociferous in demanding these, not least through the electronic comments facility which was live. They also compared the new borrower information unfavourably with that on Geac and were unhappy that we had not supplied scanners to scan in their card number since there had been light pens on the old public terminals. By the end of 1995, the missing functions had been replaced, and enhanced by self-service renewal. In 1996, networked CD-ROMs and the Web were added.

From this situation we learnt that we were not as familiar as we thought we were with the self-service requirement of users, this despite the fact that we had consulted with users about features to be included in the new system. This was probably because consultation had concentrated on new services and not on existing functionality. We had not perceived how well-used were the existing self-service functions of reservation, Dewey searching and borrower record access and that we should not have gone live without them on the replacement system. We think that now that we offer a self-service electronic comment facility from which we receive on average 100 comments per week, we are more closely in touch with users' expectations of the self-service terminals. Indeed, we take action immediately where possible to enhance self-service in response to these comments, and we shall be submitting to DS revisions to the software, e.g. the ability to delete reservations, based on regular suggestions from users.

Despite irritation at missing functionality, the users have loved the Windows-based interface on the self-service PCs, and the use of descriptive words and plain English messages, rather than codes and librarians' jargon, has made them easy to use. However, there are still two major developments needed to meet the 1996 needs of users. First, the shelf location must say exactly where the book is in any given library. We have not yet dealt with the problem of separate sequences, e.g. oversize, local studies, which do not always show in the shelf location field and this is a high priority for 1997. Second, the self-service software is excellent for the non-expert library user, but it does not offer all the sophistication of searching available to staff. We need to work together with DS to provide an expert search facility for users who understand information retrieval and expect it to be available self-service. We have also failed to inform users methodically of their personal identification numbers (PINs) and this must now be done – there are still complaints that PINs are not known, even though the help screens explain them.

Circulation

Those of us at the centre were conscious that library staff did not especially want a new circulation system. While the Geac 9000 functions were not perfect, they were familiar and fairly comprehensive. Our fear was that a new system which fulfilled our strategic ambition of providing information networking and user-friendly OPAC would not meet the level of circulation functionality expected by staff who used the Geac 9000 housekeeping software.

To Suffolk's satisfaction, not only is Galaxy 2000 a third generation system with all the associated strategic advantages, but its circulation functionality is so advanced that the library staff found it superior to that of the outgoing system. This meant that a third generation system could be brought in with the support of the staff and it ensured that we did not have to deal with a conflict between today's operational needs and tomorrow's services. We suppose that it was the development of the software in a 4GL which enabled DS to create this comprehensive circulation functionality so rapidly.

Anglia Connect and Z39.50

Anglia Connect[3] was the networked interlending cooperative of Essex, Norfolk and Suffolk libraries based on their proprietary Geac systems. To all intents and purposes, Suffolk withdrew from Anglia Connect when it moved away from a Geac system.

Anglia Connect allowed each authority to search the others' catalogues and place reservations on each others' systems. A van service carried reserved books between the counties. There was a minimum of administration, and supply times for books found in the three counties were faster than was normal for interlending.

The solution to networked interlending in the third generation system world must be the use of Z39.50 client and server software. This will enable librarians to search a number of catalogues at the same time. Development of related standards should also enable the placing of reservations. For this reason, Z39.50 is a contracted, but not delivered, feature of Galaxy 2000 and our Essex and Norfolk colleagues seem certain to specify Z39.50 for their replacement systems.

However, for Z39.50 to become usable a useful number of library services must offer it both at the client and the server end. This has not happened yet and maybe suppliers are sceptical about how important the standard is to customers. Hopefully, the British Library project ONE and work by the EARL consortium will precipitate some activity on this front. If not, maybe Anglia Connect will reform using Z39.50.

Acquisitions

On the second generation system, Suffolk was used to acquisitions software which was staff-intensive when ordering multiple copies for multiple locations. This experience led us to evaluate the acquisitions software of the tendering companies very carefully. It was important to buy software which was not only efficient in the public library environment but which would be flexible, allowing decentralized ordering and receipting if required and of course all EDI messages. In the event, the Galaxy 2000 acquisitions software was written for Suffolk (and for Aston University) and it has brought savings in staff time which would have been more dramatic if we had not been experimenting with new methods of book acquisition in the post Net Book Agreement market. Despite the irritant of some acquisitions functions still not implemented in 1997, overall the software has exceeded our most optimistic expectations.

E-mail and attachments

A prized feature of the Geac 9000 system had been the e-mail which served all 45 service points and all managerial and professional staff in Libraries & Heritage. It even reached professional colleagues in Essex and Norfolk libraries as well. This e-mail had become a key method of communication with all service points, however remote, and clearly we wanted it to be replicated on the replacement, third generation network. Unfortunately we have failed to do this and we have lived through most of 1995, all of 1996 and into 1997 without a satisfactory method of communicating rapidly. Its loss at the moment we needed it most – on installation of the new system – was a problem. It would have been easier to maintain higher morale if e-mail had not been lost.

An inadequacy of the Ingres-based system is its treatment of text. Ingres is intended for use with databases which have discrete fields in their table structures, not for the manipulation of free-form text as in text retrieval systems. This means that the Galaxy 2000 messaging system, including messages to and from borrowers, does not have word wrap (nor did Geac e-mail) or even the ability to 'return' to the next line. Galaxy messaging is rudimentary in that the message space is inadequate and it does not offer logical groups, forwarding or carbon-copy facilities. Although it has been better than nothing for the last two years, we need to install instead proper e-mail software.

DS's solution in our contract was always to provide a UNIX mail reader so we are not suggesting that they are at fault in this regard, merely that none of the solutions available in 1995 was satisfactory. The UNIX mail readers such as Elm were too complicated and unfriendly for branch staff to use. Managerial and professional staff had access to the corporate e-mail and word-processing system, so we decided, in the short-term, to live with Galaxy messaging and the corporate office system.

In 1997, it is likely that we will use the routed network to provide e-mail with attachments throughout the department, replacing both Galaxy messaging and the old corporate office system. There are now more acceptable Windows-based UNIX mail readers, e.g. Eudora and Pegasus, which all staff should be able to use easily. The solution is likely to be a combination of this with Microsoft Office products.

The loss of e-mail has been a failing of the Network '95 implementation, although it is hard to know what else could have been done realistically. The County Council routed network was not created until well into 1996, offering in practice the seamless connection from library to Libraries & Heritage headquarters to County Hall to Internet which had been anticipated in the Network '95 specification but for which the infrastructure did not then exist.

On the plus side we can now look forward to functionality which will far exceed that of Geac's e-mail: full word-processing features, the ability to send electronically A4 documents to all service points, the integration of corporate and departmental e-mail, and the opportunities to exchange mail with not only professional colleagues but also library users via the Internet. This will lead to the delivery of enquiry services and certain library housekeeping operations by e-mail.

Networked information
Experience from 1987 to 1994 of the online network reaching all service points and carrying the 8000-entry community information database, Suffolk Infolink, and JMLS's bibliographic database, LIBTEL II, made us visualize the network carrying other information (in particular, provision of the Internet, but also other databases such as the British Library OPAC and newspaper indexes on CD-ROM). The popularity of the networked catalogue in remote villages encouraged us to aim to provide other information in the same way. Clearly there are not, relatively, many users in village libraries and the number of concurrent users of networked information is going to be no more than if all the users were physically in a central library, but the benefits to those people living away from the urban centres are remarkable.

We incorporated this vision into the Network '95 specification and into the Galaxy 2000 contract. WWW and networked CD-ROMs are now carried over the network and future networked services should include CALM 2000 archive catalogue information, trading standards information, the Essex catalogue on CD-ROM and the catalogue of the University College Suffolk library.

There are two main issues about networking information, namely

- the cost of the necessary bandwidth which, particularly in a rural area where BT does not have competition from cable companies, has not come down in price to reflect the advances in technology
- the approach of CD-ROM publishers to networking which does not yet recognize the importance in rural areas of concurrent accesses as a basis for licensing.

Until there is some movement in these pricing structures, the potential for information networking in rural areas will be difficult to fulfil.

Archive cataloguing
Whereas library services had developed over the years through the application

of IT, archive services, which could benefit as much if not more more from automation, had been left to printed catalogues, card indexes and manual production systems. The Network '95 specification included a section on archives so that the processes inside the record offices could be automated and information be networked to libraries and to the outside world on the Internet.

We were very pleased when DS offered the text retrieval product CALM 2000 at a price competitive enough to allow us to purchase it.

Fine-tuning requirements

While the process of putting in a new system is in some ways a 'game of two halves' (first the period of selection of products from a choice of suppliers, then the time of working in partnership with the chosen supplier), the fine-tuning of requirements progresses in a fairly constant fashion, guided rather than punctuated by the formal decision-making process. There is a constant moving from the general to the specific until you reach the point when you know the exact character of your new library and information system, down to the last message on screen, the last configuration of functions, the final layout of the final record and the final number and location of every mouse, scanner and date stamp.

The departmental Network '95 Group, the representative group which supervised and carried out the selection and evaluation (see 'Human issues' later), divided into a significant number of small, overlapping working groups in order to narrow down the post-specification and post-selection characteristics of the system. The numerous decisions required the expertise and advice of different people and many decisions impacted on each other.

Configuration

There were many decisions to be made in preparation for the configuration of the catalogue. These included, clearly, what data should be transferred to what field, but also whether existing descriptions of the intellectual level of the book could be expanded and integrated with those available from our bibliographic record supplier, what subject indexing should be used, how annotations could be incorporated into existing records, whether inconsistencies in the catalogue should be rectified before or after data transfer, how the sound and vision records should be extended to meet the levels of retrieval demanded by the public and which fields should be indexed, whether all records should be changed to DDC 20 before or after conversion, and whether the Suffolk non-fiction subject categories should be changed before conversion. These apparently simple decisions were difficult because recommendations to change would affect many other things we did. On the other hand, decisions not to change would at best not make good use of the new software and at worst might not work with the new software.

The overwhelming lesson was that we should have dealt with some of these issues during the prime of the Geac system, not when we were busy with a new solution. Indeed, we recalled that during the Geac installation we had intended to rectify certain unsatisfactory features of the catalogue and classification after the go-live period, but we never had. This time, we have started to correct the errors in the catalogue through global editing. However, other postponed work, such as the rationalization of intellectual levels and the move of the remainder of stock to DDC 20 (now DDC 21, of course) has not yet begun and the writing of this chapter has been a reminder to start this work in the near future.

An understanding of the data structure of the new system was essential in the configuration process and our understanding could have been better. A member of staff should have been seconded to Birmingham (if it would have been possible) to learn first-hand about the structures. At the time, DS's configuration documentation was not advanced and the impact of this situation was that some decisions were made in the dark.

One of the decisions related to the organization of material into formats and media types. For example, we chose to have a format called 'books' into which we put media formats 'hardback large print books' and 'paperback large print books' as well as all other sorts of books. When, in the public catalogue, we wanted users to be able to search only large print books, we found that we could not separate large print from other books. To be able to do so, we should have made large print books a separate format. The initial decision had been made without any understanding that it would impact adversely on the public catalogue. This taught us that not only should we have understood the data structures better, but also, when using the same data for public and for staff, consideration of the needs of both sectors is necessary from the start.

We were similarly ill-equipped to use the shelf location field properly, partly because we did not foresee how important it was for staff (it is used on shelf-check messages for reservations) and for users (it tells them where in the building the item is), and partly because no-one realized how the local habit of taking books out of main sequences, e.g. local studies books, would often invalidate the information in that field. Untangling this problem is a major task for 1997.

On the whole, Suffolk staff had entered circulation information onto the Geac 9000 consistently so that the transfer of this data was more or less a matter of mapping one field to another. However, there were a few borrower cards used by staff for Home Library Service and playgroup loans and for binding which were filled out inconsistently. These were identified and staff were asked before conversion to rekey the data into the correct fields.

The Galaxy 2000 software also enabled us to exempt borrowers from certain charges in a more flexible way. This led to a change in the conditions of use of certain exempt categories at the introduction of the new software.

Budget

The budget for Network '95 had been set at the beginning of the process, in November 1993, based on ballpark costings from system suppliers and BT. It is best in local government to set a reliable figure and not to be forced to go back and to ask for more. The November 1993 budget remained realistic throughout the process and we were able to report in November 1994 that Libraries & Heritage could take out a contract for the expected levels of enhancement within the original budget.

The final permission for a five-year loan from the County Council was obtained in December 1994, just before the first year of major cuts in the Council's budget and just before a moratorium on all infrastructural development, pending the decision on the future structure of local government in Suffolk. The initial timetable and the decision to go early for a third generation system had been justified. Had it been left another three months, the project might have been delayed for at least two years.

Period of optimism

It may be stating the obvious, but even though specifying and selecting a new system is hard work, it is also an uplifting period: the time when you can plan for the medium- and long-term, and the time when you can believe that your plans can be delivered. And it is not nearly such hard work as installing the chosen product!

Installation of the new system

Summary

The Galaxy 2000 server was installed in April 1995 and the Central Bibliographical Unit started using Galaxy acquisitions at the end of April. The first five libraries went live at the beginning of May and then another few libraries every week until the last library was live at the end of June.

Most libraries were closed for two weeks, to allow not only cabling and installation but also the training of library staff for two days each (see 'Training' later). In quite a number of cases there was building work as well.

The three record offices closed for two weeks each in August and September 1996 for construction works as well as cabling and installation of hardware and software, and we started using CALM 2000 for archive cataloguing in October 1996.

Project team

For the Galaxy installation there was a three-person project team led by the Libraries & Heritage Systems Manager. The three of us worked in the same building and could meet at any time as decisions were needed. Each member of the team had his or her own responsibilities but the Systems Manager coordinated the process.

Health and safety

As early as August 1994 we began to prepare, together with the County Council's health and safety officer, for the implementation of the Health and Safety (Display Screen Equipment) Regulations 1992. During the autumn of

1994 pre-installation workplace assessments were undertaken in all libraries. These produced lists of substantial actions required to meet the Regulations and those of a less substantial nature which could be carried out immediately, e.g. the purchase of chairs that meet the Regulations. Improvements which had to wait on the installation of the new hardware (e.g. the provision of wider counters) were put onto a list which included both essential and desirable work.

The final list was costed in detail, including estimates from contractors for the installation of replacement and extended counters, and compared with the budget for health and safety work. In the event the budget (£60,000 for 41 libraries, 1 Central Bibliographical Unit, 3 record offices and Libraries & Heritage headquarters) was sufficient to fund desirable (e.g. new furniture and additional storage) as well as essential (action needed to meet the Regulations) work and everything on the list was carried out.

This work, organized by the managers who run the three library areas, was synchronized with the installation of cabling and electrical sockets by the cabling contractor and the installation of hardware by the system supplier. Project timetabling ensured that this was successful.

Attention to the physical environment ensured, amongst other things, that the hardware fitted neatly into each library. Whereas the previous installation had left holes in counters (revealed after the removal of the first generation hardware) and some uncomfortable work spaces, in 1995 staff acquired upgraded working space and some improvements to workflow and furnishings which had been on wish lists, sometimes for many years. In terms of motivation, it was useful right from the beginning to associate the new system with improvements to the working environment. The unpopularity of the installation of the second generation system in 1987 (due partly to the concurrent reduction in loan period for popular books from three to two weeks) had taught us that in 1995 there must be obvious benefits for staff.

We can now look back on a successful implementation of the Health and Safety (Display Screen Equipment) Regulations 1992. We have been carrying out post-implementation workplace assessments and are satisfied that our staff have a safe and comfortable IT environment.

Data conversion

One of the greatest risks associated with the installation was the conversion of the catalogue, borrower, community information and transaction files. The new system supplier employed software expertise with experience of the outgoing system, and the catalogue, borrowers and transactions were converted more or less successfully but with more false starts than had been allowed for in the implementation timetable. An exception to this was the 20,000 on-order reservations which on the Geac system had been attached not to the borrower record but to the title record. DS did not link this title information to the appropriate borrower records and the electronic data was lost. The situation was made more complicated because this information, which, fortunately, existed in printed form, was in three area lists. For Galaxy the three area lists had to be cumulated into one county list with all reservations in chronological order. After careful consideration, it was decided that this information should be keyed into Galaxy and staff were employed to do it. It was completed in just two weeks.

There were also problems with the conversion of the 8000 community information records due to Ingres's lack of text handling coupled with the quality of the data extracted from the outgoing system. The main problem was not to do with content, but the formatting of the text. What looked good on the Geac 9000 appeared less so in the extracted form, and by the time it was imported into Ingres some of it was out of order and misleading.

There was also the issue of editing text in an Ingres format. Each line of free-form text in the Geac system was imported as an occurrence of a field in an Ingres record. The first attempt at providing editing was unacceptable with each line having to be edited individually and any requirement for word insertion could result in having to edit each line subsequently. This has been worked around by the use of a macro which dumps all the relevant fields to a temporary text file and invoking the UNIX level text editor, JOVE. The text is then edited and upon exiting JOVE automatically and transparently reloads into the Ingres record and returns control to the Ingres application. This has worked well, but is still no substitute for a database that can handle free-form text. However, this has to be weighed against the obvious benefits that Ingres has in other areas of application development, for example fast online transaction processing and database resilience.

The outgoing system supplier, Geac, offered to quote to help with the data conversion and in retrospect this offer should have been taken up. Without good reason, we had assumed that the outgoing supplier would not facilitate our move to a competitor's system and so a decision was made not to pay for their help. In fact, Geac behaved gracefully in all respects, for which we are very grateful.

Closures
We were fortunate in that our users did not in general object to the libraries closing for two weeks. As indicated below in 'Human issues', there had been a long-term campaign to encourage users to own the new system and they were sympathetic enough to accept that it was in everyone's interests to close. They recognized that otherwise staff could not be trained satisfactorily. Often building works were going on as well. The effects were minimized by keeping some nearby libraries open, allowing three extra weeks' loan period and offering a telephone reference service as well as an emergency book collection service for anyone who needed a title urgently. We had also chosen the least busy time of year for the installation. However, some complaints were received afterwards from students and school children who had wanted to use the library and did not take up the offer of an emergency service. With hindsight this emergency service should have been made more obvious to the less assertive teenagers.

We know that most library services will not close for installation and do not think that it is necessary. Considering the work involved in removing the old system, cabling for and installing the new, training and health and safety requirements, all over a dispersed geographical area, we felt we needed to. Indeed, we even felt that there might be some benefit in doing so. By reopening with not only a superb new system but also physically improved premises, we were emphasizing a new phase in library services.

Dual running

As well as running two systems for the two-month go-live period, we also continued to let the public use any library in Suffolk that was open. It says something about how ingrained into our service is this right to borrow from one service point and return to another that we allowed it to continue during the implementation phase. It involved a lot of planning and communication with staff so that they understood how to deal with records and transactions on both systems. However, it was the technological solutions, the daily transfer of data to Galaxy that did not work smoothly and, with hindsight, this would not be done again. In future, borrowers would be allowed only to use a library on the old system or on the new, until all users were on the new system.

Timing

The schedules for installation are relentless so it is very difficult to stop a timetable once it has begun. The various contractors are scheduled, as are the trainers and trainees. Closure publicity has to go out four weeks in advance. Even beyond this, there is a human need to get the job done. Informal talks about a replacement system had been taking place since July 1993 and formal talks since November of the same year. All staff had been consulted in early 1994 about their requirements. Staff from across the department had been working on the project since January 1994. There was a momentum, an expectation for change and the project would have been damaged if the implementation been postponed or drawn out.

Network

Not only was Galaxy a new product but so was the IP routed network using a mixture of leased line and ISDN technology. The routers selected by DS for use in Suffolk were, according to their technical specification, suitable to carry high volume transactions over lines including ISDN. They were also used by IBM, albeit for batch rather than transaction processing. In the event, the network router software was not resilient and there were problems with the network for a number of months. While the most serious faults (those which affected operations) were dealt with within two or three months, underlying problems continued for around a year.

Reflecting, 18 months later, on that initial instability of the network, we do not think that the wrong routers were specified. Operating at the leading edge of the routing of transactions using ISDN, untried technology was being used. Yet ISDN, with its ability to provide high bandwidth on demand – an invaluable feature in a rural area with libraries only open a few hours a week – had so much to offer us, we had to use it. No doubt many other services of all kinds will benefit from what was learnt in Suffolk libraries.

Early in 1996, developing County Council policy required us change to our IP addressing scheme to conform to the addresses of our private Internet. All rules and guidelines on choice of the original IP addresses had been followed, but a new corporate policy was agreed at the end of 1995 and we had (and worked) to conform to it. DS Ltd undertook the address changes and the procedure went smoothly with little disruption to service.

Successes

The installation of the Network '95 project is looked back on as a success. It is a project of which elected members, staff and even some users are proud. Partly this is to be expected since Suffolk adhered to the timetable set in late 1993 and the routines of cabling and hardware installation went smoothly. However, it is also interesting because in July 1995, when all libraries were live, we were suffering the following three unacceptable problems:

- poor response times (due to a glitch in the software and cured very promptly)
- lost data (due to the back-up software and cured by the end of August)
- an unreliable network leading to regular losses of service (cured as far as operations were concerned by September).

Despite this situation, Network '95 was perceived as a success for the following three reasons:

- the project was clearly well planned
- the problems were not really apparent to users or elected members (staff could easily protect users from the problems)
- there is a honeymoon period, a time of tolerance during which staff can cope with disruption, of perhaps two or three months (during Network '95 the disruption was removed within this period of grace and hopefully customers who install Galaxy 2000 today need no period of grace because they should benefit from those who went before).

Perhaps there is a fourth reason for the perception of success: using Galaxy 2000 and latterly CALM 2000 Suffolk is providing some excellent and efficient services.

Human issues

Library staff

Apart from training, which is dealt with later, the three main issues related to staff were

- to use the expertise which exists at all levels and in all parts of the county to obtain the best possible system for Suffolk
- to ensure that all staff were motivated to view it positively
- to provide all possible help and support during implementation.

A detailed account of how of we called on the expertise of staff to achieve these objectives has already been published.[4] The main Network '95 project was supervised and carried out by the Network '95 Group, a relatively large group of 16 Libraries & Heritage staff representing all geographical areas, skills, levels of work and specialisms including the record offices. Individuals or groups wrote specific chapters for the specification and then undertook the evaluation of the tenders and fine-tuning of our requirements. For example, circulation was specified and evaluated by a group of four local library staff from across the county. They spent many hours on this, particularly during the evaluation on site of the three shortlisted products when they compared the ease of individual functions. This contrasted with the selection of the Geac 9000 when the system was evaluated and chosen by Management Team and System Centre staff only. This had no doubt contributed to the lack of initial enthusiasm for the 9000 and we wanted to avoid this in 1994. Also, by 1994, the skills of local staff in use of online systems had become so advanced that only they were really in a position to evaluate ease of use. Managers contributed to ideas for development, e.g. automated stock exchanges and global reservations, and local staff ensured that they would work in practice.

All staff were kept in touch with progress through the departmental newsletter, a separate bulletin *Real time* dedicated to all aspects of implementation, e-mails and memos, and we sent a questionnaire to all staff asking them to advise us on what they wanted from their new system. In addition, the members of the Network '95 Group were key in informing their colleagues informally of progress and feeding back questions and potential problems to the Group.

A successful part of the Geac implementation had been the timetabling of expert help to libraries for the first week or fortnight of go-live. This experience was brought forward to the Galaxy 2000 installation and replicated, although it was much more difficult to do so, because in 1987 only one library a week went live, while in 1995 about six libraries opened on the new system every week.

This support was provided by recruiting three groups of staff: trainers (see further details in 'Training'), 'staff supporters' (mostly skilled operational staff who provided expertise in libraries at go-live), and 'public supporters' (senior and middle managers who provided advice to the public at go-live and dealt with any complaints). Individuals were timetabled to each library for the first week and library staff found the support most helpful. In some places, particularly in the first group of libraries where the network had disrupted the online service, or where staff were less comfortable with the software, support was timetabled for a second week. As with the Geac implementation, this system of support was a great success and invaluable in helping local staff to gain confidence in the new product.

We found that staff in many libraries reached an emotional low perhaps five or six weeks after go-live. As has already been said, the system was not thoroughly reliable until the end of August 1995, although the disruptions were not particularly evident to users so they did not create the pressure. We are not sure that this explains the dips in morale which occurred at about the six week period because staff recovered their equanimity well before the end of August. Perhaps it had more to do with the emotional investment in the implementation which created the 'high' necessary to change systems, inevitably to be followed by a 'low' at some point.

It is easy to write up the issues affecting local staff and to take for granted the huge amount of work and pressure incurred by system centre staff. The move to a third generation system demanded from them new skills and the redundancy of many second generation skills of which they were justifiably proud (we think that on this occasion this issue of skill loss affected system centre staff even more than library staff). This has not been helped by DS's minimalist approach to system centre training.

Beyond this, the number of hours worked by system centre staff during the go-live period was very high. We are very grateful for their professional attitude which always concentrated on the needs of local library staff first, and their own last.

Library users

As mentioned earlier, library users could be very critical of the first and second generation systems, until the Geac 9000 became stable, when the customers became rather fond of it. In 1994, the aim from the outset was to ensure that users would like the third generation system. We believed that with careful and thoughtful planning, this could be achieved.

The first step was to keep staff involved in the selection process, since most messages reach users from local staff.

The second move was to invite the potential suppliers to demonstrate the seven tendered systems to the public, each in one of seven of the larger libraries. This was a revealing exercise in two ways. First, the users were more demanding of their new system than we had anticipated. A summary of their requirements is included in Figure 2.5 (p.54). Second, it seemed to us that the suppliers' representatives were not used to dealing with the public. Some were very loath to allow the keyboard or mouse into the hands of a user. There are more serious implications to this than sympathetic amusement at seeing sales people operating in a new environment. It demonstrated to us just how many

OPACs had been designed not for the public but for the librarians who attend the exhibitions and buy the software. Librarians make poor substitutes for the public in specifying and evaluating OPACs and we would urge other library services to involve potential suppliers with their users. We are now developing with DS the public interface for CALM 2000 and will involve record office users at the appropriate stage.

Library users were provided with a preclosure leaflet explaining why the libraries had to close and what the new system would do, and then another leaflet upon opening, telling them in more detail about functions available. In both leaflets, care was taken to underestimate features, so that users could be surprised and pleased with the services, rather than disappointed.

Each library was staffed during its go-live with senior or middle managers – including the Director and Assistant Directors – to help people to use the new public terminals and to ensure that local staff did not have to deal with any complaints. On the whole, users needed little help with using the public terminals, which are intuitive, have on-screen commands and use plain English. There was some confusion with the PC keyboards which boot to Number Lock On. This confused people when they tried to use certain arrow keys. To counter this, notices were put out explaining it. However, it was decided that in general PC keyboards are now a standard and that users would benefit from learning how to use them. As stated earlier, there was also confusion about PINs and disappointment that some functions were not operational immediately.

Since mid-1995, users have had the use of an electronic comments system through which we receive about 100 comments each week. This is a method by which OPAC users communicate directly to us their complaints about and aspirations for the service. They have provided the first news of bugs introduced and have given us clear guidance on future developments. This facility enables Suffolk to keep up-to-date with the opinions of the users of the self-service functions and thus provides invaluable feedback. Figure 2.6 provides some examples of feedback.

Elected members

Suffolk has been for the two decades of our library IT systems an authority which approves of and funds IT. In this culture, we expected that the County Council would support the implementation of a third generation system, providing the department could fund it.

We have the funding infrastructure to finance the maintenance and renewal of the IT systems: there is a revenue budget and a 'repairs and renewals' fund. We found that the third generation systems provided more value for money than the previous systems, primarily because the costs of hardware, hardware maintenance and communications have reduced in price significantly. It was possible to show members that the budget was sufficient, that they would obtain value for money, including archive automation, within the same budget and that the public, as shown in Figure 2.5, were demanding improved IT services.

'The new computer system is a lot better than the old one. It is easier to use and has some good facilities like being able to renew your books and reserve books without bothering the library staff. I enjoy the new system and hope CD-ROM[5] is made available in all libraries not just the larger ones.'

Felixstowe user, 29 August 1996

'To the people at library HQ: do you think that there is any way you could let library users use the Internet and World Wide Web[6] or some kind of encyclopaedia, etc.? Also, how about some kind of bulletin board for library users?'

Mildenhall user, 9 August 1996

'I think the service you offer is very good. One minor quibble is that it does not seem possible to cancel a reservation from home and to do that recently I had to go to my local library. Not really a big problem I agree.'

Aldeburgh user, 11 July 1996

'Thank you for getting the modem dial-in system working ... '

Woodbridge and dial-in user, 18 June 1996

'Any chance of changing this system so that, for example, I can change my name, address and 'phone number details without having to (a) queue up and (b) take up the valuable time of your staff?'   *Ipswich user, 17 May 1996*

'Thanks for good work of having the facility to reserve which ever books we like. The only disappointment is that I can't delete the book I reserve by mistake.'   *Haverhill user, 2 May 1996*

'I have found the service very useful. I am new to the area, and expected a lower class of service, but was surprised at the use of technology. It has made my visits much more enjoyable and the time spent bothering staff has been greatly reduced.'   *Woodbridge user, 1 May 1996*

'I appreciate the cost implications, but additional Viewpoint terminals would be welcome. Alternatively, would it be possible to arrange the system so that those using the system would have a limit to the time they were able to use the terminal, e.g. five minutes maximum, no return for another five minutes?'   *Ipswich user, 24 May 1996*

'Dear Mr. Where this electronic message ends up, I am just writing to say how pleased I am with the work you and all the other Suffolk library employees have put into this computer system ... I am especially impressed with your new renewal system as it saves my much needed time by meaning that I do not need to queue up ... '   *16-year-old Beccles user, 23 May 1996*

Fig. 2.6 *Examples of self-service electronic comments*

Libraries & Heritage Committee members were also invited to the seven public demonstrations of the tendering systems so that they could question the companies' representatives and assure themselves that the County Council was obtaining value for money. The elected members were assured of the rigour of the project and decided to finance it.

Record office staff

The issues relating to record office staff have been both similar and different. The issue of 'ownership' of the project has been the same and the CALM 2000 Group, representing most interests in the record offices, has supervised, in close partnership with Hampshire Record Office, the development of the product, particularly its ability to deal with the archival concept of hierarchy. However, many record staff were not familiar with computers. This has created significant training and coaching demands, together with the need to tackle fears about new technology. This is being done by dealing with key staff on a one-to-one basis and, so far, things are going smoothly.

Training

One human resources issue stands head and shoulders above all others when implementing a system – such as training. While everyone will willingly acknowledge that fact, it seems strange, even perverse, that companies offering systems still do not accord this subject sufficient priority and resources; and those that do focus on implementation and give far less attention to on-going needs. While the Network '95 Group was unanimous in its choice of Galaxy 2000 as the best solution for Suffolk's overall needs, DS's options for training were not as impressive as some of their competitors'.

When dealing with the training for the Geac system in 1987–8 Suffolk had opted for a training team of five staff to work full-time for 18 months (on secondment from their usual jobs) in a centrally-located dedicated training centre. The latter housed 15 terminals in three rooms. The training programme lasted three days and was delivered during the closure period for each library. All handouts and manuals to support the training were written by the training team, for although Geac provided a great deal of documentation it was compiled by programmers and unsuitable for use by operational staff. Further, it needed not only to be tailored to the functionality being supplied but also to reflect Suffolk's policies and practices in specific and important areas.

That a little over 400 staff were trained to migrate from a non-automated process to a fully-integrated system over the period with a 'failure rate' (i.e. those staff who were unable to cope and had to be redeployed) of just 2% was a source of immense satisfaction. Obviously, it was not a straightforward process and pitfalls and problems were encountered. Not surprisingly, perhaps, those of us who survived hoped in our weaker moments that we would not be around to deal with the implementation of the next system. Some of us were and we were able to use the lessons learned to inform the process.

Galaxy 2000 was approached in the knowledge that the best elements from the Geac 9000 training process could be employed – it was clear where problems were most likely to arise and there was an awareness of the shortcomings of suppliers with regard to training. What had not been envisaged nine years earlier was that, if it had to be done again, it would have to be completed within just seven weeks.

Despite the stresses and strains that the job might involve, an internal advertisement for potential Galaxy 2000 trainers attracted over 30 applicants. We had already decided that eight would be required. This was based upon the need to train up to 60 staff in any one week across a variety of service points, for although a dedicated training centre would still be used, it could not accommodate the numbers involved in the timescale available. Therefore, a range of training venues was needed. This, in turn, necessitated the recruitment of trainers from diverse locations who had not only the required skills but also ready access to transport. Fortunately, five trainers remained from the Geac experience and so only three new members were required to make up the team.

Having assembled the trainers, our first task was to get DS Ltd to train them. Despite being aware of Suffolk's timetable well in advance, the training was not available until the week before the first library closure. Two full days at DS Ltd's offices in Ferndown, Dorset proved adequate. We had hoped for a dedicated training suite but found a seemingly makeshift centre. We had to make do with two trainers per terminal (i.e. hands-on training for trainers was limited) and were faced with getting to grips with the circulation software of another authority – which kept going down. As a result, we had to take what we had gained back to Suffolk and, basically, taught ourselves the rest.

Before the trainer training, the training process had already been agreed as being based on Suffolk's model for Geac 9000 training. Given that the one training centre in itself was insufficient for the task, there was a discussion with DS Ltd about the use of the larger libraries during their closure periods. Not all libraries needed to be used – just a select number which would have clusters of four or five terminals readily available. With different groups of libraries, each closing for two weeks, it seemed reasonable that we might identify locations in each group where training could take place. DS Ltd were approached on this basis and their head of engineering proved most helpful. Together, we identified which locations were required, how many terminals were needed and precisely when.

The best laid plans . . . No sooner had the planning started than DS Ltd explained that they could not, after all, guarantee the availability of terminals as we had agreed. This was for reasons which, in all fairness, were not so unreasonable – they were not to know where they might encounter problems and they needed the flexibility to move their engineering staff around should difficulties be found. Thus, if they discovered a cabling or other problem at a site where they had guaranteed training terminals, they maintained it was pointless for their staff to sit tight while they waited for say, BT to fix the fault. They would need to move staff to a different site where progress *could* be made and then return to carry on once the cause of the delay had been rectified.

Accepting their situation, we put it to DS that this left it open to all sorts of potential problems – the most serious being that, at worst, we might have staff who could not be trained before their library reopened. The solution to this situation proved more effective than we might have hoped. Within Suffolk's Headquarters, a meeting room was converted to a stand-by training suite with six terminals. It was intended for use as a back-up, but eventually it functioned as an on-going training location and, just as crucially, as a software testing site.

Having identified the trainers and training venues, the remaining challenge was how to fit the training of all the staff into the seven weeks – not just training for circulation, but for acquisitions as well.

Initial advice from DS suggested that the system was so easy to use and so intuitive, that a single day's training per person would suffice. Although we did not agree with this, we came to the conclusion that the circulation software was, indeed, overwhelmingly more straightforward than the Geac system staff had been used to operating. No longer was there the major requirement to try to remember TLA (three-letter abbreviation) commands. However, staff would have to 'unlearn' their Geac-based skills and knowledge before they could move to a new situation which, while not strictly Windows-based, still used pop-up boxes, drop-down menus, function keys and the like, and to a PC environment far removed from dumb terminals.

There were also a number of policy and practice matters which had to be included. When the Geac system was implemented it was accompanied by a whole raft of policy changes which added the best part of a day to the training required for its introduction. We chose not to do this for Galaxy 2000, but there were some unavoidable issues (especially those deriving from the requirements of legislation) although, happily, the elements to be incorporated were fairly minimal.

Looking at staff numbers, days available and issues to be covered, a series of key questions had to be addressed and some difficult decisions taken. It was clear how much time there was and the number of staff to be trained. It was also clear that staff had to know what they were doing when service points reopened and yet it would not be possible to cover everything they would need. Asking staff to run a new system without all of the knowledge they might need was, on the face of it, an unhappy position to be in. If all staff were to be trained in the time available, only a two-day programme could be offered. Even that would depend on DS and ourselves encountering few problems during the implementation.

The approach, given the various training needs, was to cut the training to those elements of functionality that were absolutely essential. This might arguably have been sensible in any event, but anything not covered during the two days would then have to be covered later and at a time when libraries were not closed. This was, in effect, generating an 'implementation training programme: phase II' for all staff. Having looked at the staff involved, a strict priority was determined to focus on staff dealing directly with customers. This meant that professional (team) librarians, managers, mobile library staff and so on were not included in the early training schedules. Some found this uncomfortable but we found most of them were trained within the period, which was a bonus for morale.

The trainers were experienced staff who themselves work daily with customers. During the delivery of training programmes, they were able to ensure that staff being trained knew precisely how to deal with situations which might be encountered. Fortunately not one trainer went sick during the implementation period. Downtime was encountered and a number of problems resulted from difficulties experienced by DS Ltd during the installation of hardware, but our best laid plans combined with our experience of the Geac installation meant that we knew what to cancel, when to reschedule and how to move staff to different training locations at short notice. The need for flexibility cannot be overemphasized. That we ourselves and staff being trained were prepared for this meant that the whole process went very well.

Documentation to accompany the training was minimal. In Geac days, the trainers spent weeks preparing comprehensive handouts and, ultimately, five detailed manuals. The latter proved impossible to maintain on any reasonable basis and for Galaxy 2000 we had to reduce the paperwork to a manageable amount and format.

A 15-page 'quick start' to circulation functionality was produced which covered basics. This was accompanied by half a dozen handouts. It was minimalist, but it worked. It was more than sufficient to support the training and for staff to use as an aide-memoire when back in the workplace.

Post-implementation, just one formal handbook was compiled. Even this was minimal, aimed at fleshing out the training material. The big advantage of producing this after the first training had been completed (about three months later) was that it gave staff and trainers time to discover short-cuts and ways of doing things which required far fewer keystrokes than documentation from DS suggested. It also enabled trainers, particularly, to identify elements of functionality which were not worth using. This is not to deny the value of these redundant functions to other library services, but the software allows tasks to be carried out in any number of ways and it really requires some degree of experience of applying the functionality to your own situation before you can identify how best and how effectively it can be operated. By leaving the manual for a while, it was possible to incorporate best practice, staff suggestions and software 'fixes' which had been applied to problems encountered during implementation. The result was a handbook which is genuinely user-friendly, one valued as having a real use and adding to what staff already knew. It is not something they put on a shelf and then forget.

Phase II of the training started almost immediately after the last library migrated to Galaxy 2000. Phase I had covered basic circulation. It had also, for a dozen staff in the Central Bibliographical Unit (which deals with the ordering, cataloguing and receipting of stock), included training in acquisitions. This was a fairly straightforward process which involved acquisitions specialists from DS Ltd training four key staff in the Unit who then trained others on-site.

Phase II, for all staff, required attendance on a half-day circulation 'refresher' programme, a half-day course on catalogue searching (as the Galaxy 2000 basic course could only, within the time, deal with simple techniques) and then a half-day looking at the customer's view of Galaxy 2000 – particularly important since the provision of terminals for users is part of Suffolk's self-service philosophy and there is so much that customers can do. Not unreasonably during the implementation period staff focused on their own situations, and so a post-implementation dedicated opportunity to look at Viewpoint (the self-service facility) was particularly valuable.

All in all, the training went very well. The previous Geac 9000 training experience had enabled us to identify problem areas and little cropped up that we had not encountered previously or had not anticipated. If anything, we were pleasantly surprised – most especially by how well and how easily staff took to Galaxy 2000. The 'failure rate' was 0% – some staff did have top-up/refresher sessions but nobody was unable to cope.

Since the completion of all elements within both phase I and phase II, on-going training has, by and large, been restricted to new staff. Existing staff have been able to cope with upgrades and major 'bug fix' releases through the use of newsletters and additional paperwork supported by local training. Indeed, the philosophy and practice centres on training being delivered as close to the workplace as possible – not 'sitting next to Nelly', but a far more proactive and constructive approach that focuses on cost-effective training solutions.

Suffolk has a proven track-record when it comes to IT training generally and library system training in particular. In Geac days that recognition was reflected in a variety of ways including lectures, visits, advice to others and the selling of training services. The Galaxy 2000 experience has consolidated and built on that reputation and we are very pleased that it has been recognized: the manager coordinating the training has been made a Member of the Institute of IT Training, and Libraries & Heritage itself is destined for formal recognition as well. We are anxious to progress and develop still further. Until library and information system suppliers can deliver training when required, as required and fully supported by customer-friendly documentation, we shall set our own training standards and ensure that our staff receive the best possible training and support to enable them to exploit, in this case, Galaxy 2000 to the benefit of our customers.

Conclusions

Over a period of 20 years our automation decisions have followed a consistent path towards more efficiency, more effectiveness, more choice, new services and new methods of delivery. The dreams of fast request supply times, networked information and self-service transactions were there years ago, but only the third generation open systems have the potential to deliver in any kind of integrated way – beyond departmental and county boundaries. Open systems were being discussed many years ago, but they did not exist in practice. At last they do and, combined with cheap and powerful hardware, the possibilities for library services are dramatic.

This chapter has summarized what the third generation technology can already deliver in Suffolk, namely fast production of elegant application software, networking of the Web and CD-ROMs across the Libraries & Heritage wide-area network, Suffolk catalogue and self-service transactions on the Web, Suffolk intranet and other departments' information available across the Libraries & Heritage network, word-processing and e-mail integrated from branch library to headquarters to County Council to the world, staff handbooks and guidance on the intranet, electronic discussion groups for staff and service delivery over the Web, and so on.

There remain two major areas where we want to develop services but so far have been restricted. We want to network much greater quantities of information including multimedia, but this requires wide bandwidth at an affordable price. Second, we are keen to cooperate with other public libraries, creating and sharing information and using standards to improve services for our users. Suffolk has joined the EARL consortium to work with the other partners to achieve just this.

It is not clear whether the traditional library suppliers will meet the future demands of libraries and library users. Library software divides into housekeeping applications and information provision. Although, in the past housekeeping modules have been most important to librarians, in the future information retrieval will become at least as influential, with the management of diverse information on the network and third-party products crucial. There is the option to develop these skills in-house, contract them out to new markets or look to the traditional library supply sector to offer information management on the networks. We shall see whether the traditional suppliers are culturally able to respond to this challenge.

It is possible that public libraries are facing a new golden age, albeit temporary, recognized in the UK by such government reports as *Government direct*[7] and *Reading the future*[8] to be the sources of networked public information, free at the point of use, for those who cannot afford, or do not have the skills, to access it at home.

Some readers will say that there will be no golden age because libraries are not resourced sufficiently, that other players will meet the demand for networked public information free at the point of use and that libraries will dwindle into book depositories with declining use. Although pessimism is understandable at a time of cuts in library budgets, there is reason for optimism: decreasing costs of systems, recognition of libraries' role by political parties, public demand for networked information, alternative sources of funding, the cost-effectiveness of public library budgets and, above all, the technology itself which can carry out the things which in the past we could only have wished for.

References

1 Pachent, G., 'Network '95: choosing a third generation automated information system for Suffolk Libraries & Heritage', *Program*, **30** (3), July 1996, 213–28.
2 Heseltine, R., 'Choosing in the dark: strategic issues in the selection of library automation systems', *ITs news*, **27**, April 1993, 13–18.
3 *Library and information briefings*, **37/38**, December 1992, 24.
4 Pachent, G., op. cit.
5 Networked CD-ROMs are now available in all 41 libraries.
6 The WWW is already networked to six libraries and record offices. Roll-out to all other libraries is due in 1997.
7 *Government direct: a prospectus for the delivery of government services*, Cm 3438, Cabinet Office, 1996.
8 *Reading the future: a review of public libraries in England*, Department of National Heritage, 1997.

3 Replacing Geac 9000 and Dynix 'Classic' systems with Dynix Horizon

Dennis Nicholson, Jean Shaw and George Geddes

Introduction

The University of Strathclyde received its charter in 1964, but it traces its history back to 1796 when it was originally founded as Anderson's Institution in the middle of the first Industrial Revolution. Until April 1993, the University had four faculties: Science, Engineering, Business and Arts. After that date, following a merger between Jordanhill College of Education and the University, it acquired a fifth faculty, Education, and became, as a result, Scotland's largest University, with over 56,000 students. Jordanhill College has been training teachers for over 70 years as one of the largest and most highly respected institutions of its kind in the UK. As a result of the merger, the University now has two campuses – John Anderson Campus in the centre of Glasgow and Jordanhill Campus, approximately five miles away. The central campus has four libraries, the 'main library' or Andersonian, the Law Library, The Fleck Chemistry Library and the Business Information Centre. In total, the five libraries generate issues of 880,000 a year. The database size is 550,000 titles, including 8000 serials and 750,000 items. This includes 8000 serial titles, 4000 of which are current subscriptions. New orders run at 25,000 a year and items catalogued run at a similar level. This case study details the Library's attempt to put in place a library management system and associated automation and networking strategy for the new century – or, at any rate, the systems staff's perspective on that attempt.

In September 1994, the University invited library systems suppliers to tender for the replacement of its Library systems – at that time, a Geac 9000 GLIS system at the main John Anderson Campus and a Dynix 'Classic' system at the Jordanhill Campus – operating under the open procedure of the EC Procurement Regulations. Tenders were received in November 1994 and a decision was taken to purchase the Dynix Horizon library system in late February/early March 1995, the aim being to merge the databases and install a single integrated replacement system by the beginning of the 1995–6 academic year. This was an ambitious timescale – overly ambitious as it turned out – for what amounted to two system replacements, a database merge and the implementation of an entirely new automation and networking strategy. However, the scheduling of the process was never really a matter of choice, being largely determined by factors outwith the Library's control. One major factor was financial considerations relating to the availability of funds and the increasingly prohibitive cost of annual maintenance charges on the older systems. Another factor was the need to upgrade, extend and integrate user facilities and associated networked services sooner rather than later. There was also the need to merge the database of what had previously been Jordanhill College of Education Library into the main University database.

This being so, it would be incorrect to say that choosing to attempt such an ambitious programme in such a short timescale was a mistake, despite the problems we subsequently encountered (a mix of conversion problems, implementation timetable slippages and late delivery of new software releases that mean we will not get the full range of functionality ordered until the end of 1997), for we did not really have a valid alternative choice and we embarked on the project knowing it would be difficult to complete it in such a short period of time. It would also be incorrect to say that we failed to recognize that there were risks involved in choosing a new and relatively untried product (as Dynix Horizon was then, in 1995). We believed, however, not not only that the risks were outweighed by the potential benefits in respect of the implementation of our new automation and networking strategy sooner rather than later (a view which we still hold), but also (correctly as it turned out) that we had in place sufficient safeguards to carry us through any period of difficulty, both in terms of written agreements on payment schedules, commitments on eventual delivery of functionality and coverage of any on-going old system maintenance payments in the event of installation slippage, and in respect of a company with the resources and the reputation to be relied upon to honour such agreements.

This is not to suggest that there were no useful lessons to be learnt from the difficulties encountered during the installation process. On the contrary, we learnt a number of things of value not only in respect of our own approach to such exercises in future, and to others about to embark on similar system replacement programmes, but also, perhaps, to the companies who supply and install library systems. In particular:

- our suspicion that the timescale was too short to allow for mishaps was confirmed, the lesson being not that such projects should never be undertaken if the need arises, but that, in future, forward planning should seek to ensure that more time is available to enable a more leisurely implementation
- we learnt, unfortunately, that the safeguards the Library had put in place were necessary, but also, fortunately, that they were, by and large, effective (e.g. we had in place an agreement that the system supplier would meet old system maintenance costs in the event of slippage, and we had a system supplier large enough to be able to do so and reliable enough to be willing to continue to do so despite the costs)
- we learnt that it is all too easy to underestimate the extent to which automated library management systems now permeate all areas of library work, how much confusion some members of staff would suffer when faced both with a new system and an entirely new kind of interface, the level of re-edu-

cation that would be required for all staff and the level of help from systems staff that would be necessary

- we learnt that new software products are not just new to the world at large, they are also new to the company developing them, a fact that can (and probably will) cause problems during early implementations of any new product.

At the time of writing (late 1996) most of these early problems appear to have been weathered. Nevertheless, it is an undeniable fact that although, on the one hand, the Library now has in place the core of its new automation and networking strategy and a stable system with many attractive features that is a springboard for future developments, on the other hand, various parts of library functioning did suffer significant levels of disruption during the process, and some parts of the promised functionality are not now due for delivery until late 1997. Whether or not we were wrong to choose a relatively untried system, especially given the short timescale for implementation, is open to discussion and readers will no doubt wish to consider the details given here and make their own judgments. The conclusions of the systems staff involved are that

- our various aims were worth meeting
- we now have good reason to suppose that we will have met all of our aims by the end of 1997 (although we also said we wanted to meet them without significant disruption!)
- there is no evidence to suggest that we could have met our aims at all, and certainly not in this timescale, had any other path been taken, nor that any other path would not have entailed similar difficulties.

These conclusions are argued at the end of this chapter, but different groups of professionals, both within and outwith Strathclyde University, will have their own different perspectives on the issue. Those reading the account as a preparation for a system replacement of their own are reminded that the account will certainly be out-of-date by the time it is published and read. Horizon will have moved on in terms of both functionality and design, e.g. a switch from OS/2 to Windows 95 and/or Windows NT is planned during 1997.

Automation at Strathclyde – historical context to current strategy

Introduction
The selection and installation of Dynix Horizon ushered in a third era of automation at Strathclyde University Library and represented the implementation of a strategy for information systems development formulated partly as a result of earlier experience, partly as a result of information systems development in the wider world, and partly as a result of the implications of the merger with Jordanhill College. The developments described later in this chapter are

best evaluated in the context of an understanding of the strategy itself and the historical and other environments which helped give rise to it: locally written systems at Strathclyde University Library pre-1985, pre-merger systems environments at both institutions (1985–94) and the post-merger environment.

Locally written systems: Strathclyde University, pre-1985

Prior to the installation of the Geac system in 1986 and of the other smaller systems described below, Strathclyde University had in place an ALS technology based, but locally-written (and much loved) circulation system. Other smaller locally-created systems, e.g. for the production of catalogue cards and short loan course lists, had also been in use. In addition, the Library had, until switching to OCLC in 1985, been a member of the Scottish Library Cooperative Automation Project (SCOLCAP) cooperative cataloguing scheme. It is neither necessary nor useful to describe this period comprehensively or in detail. It is, however, necessary to mention it in passing, because it did give rise to two factors which continue to influence the automation environment on the one hand, and the current strategy on the other.

First, although the University had 99% or more of its stock in the OPAC after 1986, and all of the records in the Geac system were UKMARC format, the database was an amalgam of earlier catalogues: in particular, the non-MARC 'catalogue 1', the UKMARC SCOLCAP database and the USMARC OCLC records held on Geac in UKMARC, each with its own particular idiosyncracies – a factor which inevitably increased the complexity of the recent conversion even without the (sensible and necessary) decision to switch from UKMARC to USMARC and, of course, the need to incorporate the Jordanhill database (which had its own unique characteristics).

Second, although the locally-written systems, and in particular the circulation system, were found to be flexible and adaptable in ways that no 'off the shelf' mass-market system could ever be, software maintenance and, more crucially, software development, being dependant on limited local staffing resources and largely cut off from other product developments in the wider world, was slow and woefully inadequate in comparison to what was possible in the commercial sector – a factor which influenced the decision to purchase an 'off the shelf' commercial system in 1986 and, subsequently, in 1994, the development of a strategy which sought to find a sustainable 'half-way house' between the advantages of the 'off the shelf' approach on the one hand and those of the more flexible and locally adaptable home-grown system on the other.

Pre-merger systems environment at Strathclyde University

The Library produced its operational requirement (OR) and invited tenders during 1994. Just prior to this (November 1993), the description of IT-related services summarized below was presented to the University as part of an attempt to secure finance for the replacement exercise. Non-Geac elements were included for two reasons. First, it was important that the University recognize that IT services were widespread in the Library and that only the Geac system was being replaced. Second, it was intended that the replacement process, once agreed, would be used as an opportunity to introduce a new automation and networking environment which would enable the interpretation of many of these non-Geac systems, thereby laying the ground work for a future integrated approach to information systems developments.

Overview

Information and communications technologies are used extensively to support the public and the administrative functions of the Library. In hardware terms, this support is centred on

- The Geac 9000 minicomputer, with
  a three processor Geac 9000 with 16MB memory

number of disk drives	=	11 x 340 MB
number of staff terminals	=	35
number of user terminals	=	35
number of network channels	=	20
total terminal capacity	=	100

  one tape drive
  600 Ipm system printer
  three control terminals
  five screen printers
  four back-up microcomputers
- over 70 staff and user access microcomputers, one of which is a multi-user interlibrary loans system
- over 40 KCS links from Library microcomputers to the campus X.25 network and from there to JANET, PSS and other networks
- over 30 ethernet links to the Library CD network, the University backbone ethernet to which it is attached, and from there to the Internet.

Only the Geac 9000-based services require replacement. Information on the other aspects of IT in the library has been provided partly for the sake of completeness, partly because there will be a requirement to integrate some parts of the non-Geac IT facilities with those of the replacement system, and partly because the new system may have modules which will replace some non-Geac facilities.

IT-supported functions in the Library may be summarized under the following headings.

Geac 9000

This provides

- an online public access catalogue accessible from Library terminals and from campus network terminals (over 99% of bookstock and all serials holdings are recorded in the catalogue, which may be searched by author, title, author and title, subject, class number, keyword and Boolean combination; circulation status, on-order information and user-specific borrowing information are also provided)

- a library information service for users
- a cataloguing module, interfaced with the OCLC database
- a circulation module, with short loan and materials booking and circulation back-up facilities
- an acquisitions module, supporting book, serial and other ordering, serials check-in and financial control
- stock control
- automatic module for control of overnight jobs and other peripheral processes.

OCLC

OCLC provides reduced cataloguing costs through online access to the largest shared cataloguing database in the world. Use of this means that only 4% of new acquisitions are now catalogued in-house. The remainder are brought from OCLC, processed in various ways to make them suitable for local requirements and added to the Geac database in an overnight process. As a result of a switch to OCLC in 1985, the Library was able to reallocate significant staff resources to information services. Access to OCLC is via JANET and, for back-up, PSS.

Interlibrary loans

Control of transmission of interlibrary loans requests is managed using a microcomputer-based three terminal multi-user system produced by Lancaster University. This system allows direct communication of requests to BLDSC over JANET. It runs under the Pick operating system and does not, at present, interface with the main library system.

The Library CD-ROM network

This is based on one network server, two optical servers, and two CD-ROM towers. It utilizes Novell networking software and Optinet CD-ROM networking software and is connected to the campus backbone ethernet. It provides access from most user-access microcomputers to networked CD-ROMs (nine at present, but expected to grow) and also to a hypertext-based guide to IT services in the Library. Access is possible from departmental machines connected to the backbone ethernet, provided that various other technical requirements are met.

The Library Systems Division is working on the installation of client/server access to Internet resources on the network. This is already available from a microcomputer in the System Division office and is likely to be provided on user-access microcomputers in the next six months. This will greatly enhance user-access to Internet-based services, allowing multimedia retrieval and display and a number of other enhancements via a GUI interface.

User-access microcomputers

There are over 30 user-access microcomputers in the Library and its satellites. These support a wide range of information service functions:

- network access to other library OPACs on JANET, the Internet, and other networks
- network access to a wide and growing range of academic resources on JANET and the Internet via the BUBL Information Service, NISS and other networked facilities, e.g. CWISs at other universities
- network access to CD-ROMs and disk-based services on the CD network
- access to CD-ROMs available in the Library but not yet networked
- access to a range of other machine-readable information sources available in the Library
- access to facilities available on other machines on campus, including online access to the Jordanhill catalogue, an additional route to the Andersonian catalogue and access to Library information held in VAX Notes.

Online service

The Library's online information retrieval service provides access to data held on thousands of commercial databases world-wide. Each satellite library has an online service microcomputer, the main library has several. Short simple searches are provided free, more complex searches are charged for.

Staff microcomputers

These support a wide range of functions, including

- financial reporting
- systems support (Geac, CD network, etc.)
- staff CD-ROM access
- online service logging and invoice processing
- word processing
- statistics logging and reporting
- reference work
- e-mail (via the VAX cluster)
- graphic design
- staff access to the various information services used by users (see above)
- spreadsheet use (subject breakdown of issue statistics)
- equipment and software inventory
- desktop publishing facilities.

VAX-based functions

The University's VAX cluster is utilized as follows:

- a networked version of the Geac library information database is provided via the VAX Notes facility

- access to the Jordanhill library OPAC is possible
- an in-house program enables users to send telex requests from their offices to the library telex service via e-mail
- e-mail is used widely for current awareness, communication with other universities and communication with the Computer Centre and other departments.

SALSER

The library is a partner in a cooperative project which has the aim of producing a network-accessible union catalogue of serials holdings in Scottish academic libraries. The project is called SALSER and is an initiative of the Scholar group. The service will probably be based on a combination of the WAIS and Gopher software technologies.

The various services described in this summary influenced the strategy employed in choosing and implementing a replacement system and, hence, the choice of the system itself, a particular concern being to provide a computing and networking environment within which, over time, these various services could be integrated, then expanded and developed in a coherent way. The following are other elements of significance in this respect.

- The CATRIONA project, which took place in the second half of 1994. This joint project with Napier University Library investigated the feasibility of a distributed catalogue of Internet resources based on MARC, Z39.50 and library OPACs, which offered simultaneous access to records of hardcopy and electronic resources and delivery of electronic resources to the desk top via these records.
- The University environment. In particular, the imminent demise of X.25, the continuing move towards a distributed and networked computing environment, and the movement of administrative automated processes to an SQL compliant ORACLE-based environment.
- The desire to move away from proprietary systems such as the Geac 9000 and to install modular flexible and safer alternatives.

Pre-merger systems environment at Jordanhill College

The position as regards automation and networking at Jordanhill was described in a similar paper, the main points being as follows.

Library automation

A Dynix automated library system was installed at Jordanhill Library in September 1989. The system is based on an Ultimate 3030 minicomputer with 4MB of main memory and 48 ports.

number of disk drives	=	2 x 510MB
number of staff terminals	=	21
number of OPAC terminals	=	19

one tape drive
one system printer
four auxiliary printers

Currently, the system is on Dynix release 135 and the modules in use are

* cataloguing
* acquisitions
* circulation
* serials
* reserve book room.

There is a contract to receive the Community Information module but this has been deferred for financial and staffing reasons. A further Dynix module, Media Scheduling, is not under consideration at the moment.

CD-ROM

CD-ROM searching has been available in Jordanhill Library since 1987. A new standalone workstation was purchased in 1992, based on a Dell 325SX PC and a Toshiba CD-ROM drive. To cope with increasing demand, a small Novell network was installed in 1993. This consists of an Optech/Toshiba 8-drive tower, optical and network servers (Viglen Genie Professional 4DX33), Allied Telesis multiport repeater and four workstations (Viglen Genie Executive 3SX25). Databases currently available are

* networked
  – ERIC (4 users)
  – PsycLit (single user)
  – SPORT Discus (single user)
* standalone
  – MEDLINE
  – NERIS (ceased publication).

Other IT provision

The Information Services Librarian conducts online searches on BLAISE and DIALOG from her own PC. The Periodicals/ILL Librarian uses ARTtel to transmit ILL requests. The Systems Librarian, the Media Librarian and the Information Services Librarian have PCs with connections to the library Dynix machine and the University network. The Library enquiry desk also has a PC with Dynix, network and modem access.

Student access

During normal library opening hours, users can have access to BBC Master and Archimedes computers. Ten Apple Macs, with printing facilities, are also available. These are the responsibility of the Computer Education Section, though located in the Media Library.

Aims at Jordanhill at the time included

- making Jordanhill CD-ROM network available on the University network
- installing Dynix OPAC for those with visual disabilities
- merging with the Andersonian system.

A major aim was to make access to JANET widely available to Jordanhill users, something the library staff had wanted to do for some time but for which they had been unable to obtain Computing Unit support.

Post-merger environment

Jordanhill College merged with the University on 1 April 1993. Library staff had been in discussion for some time prior to the merger and had agreed that no immediate action could be taken on merging computing systems. The systems and databases could be merged at system replacement time which was only about two years off. Some preparatory work specific to systems merger was undertaken during this period, e.g. Jordanhill Library began using the OCLC service used by the University and, as a result, switched to MARC cataloguing, and there was some integration of the two CD networks. Most of the work done in this period, however, related to an integration or harmonization of library practices on the two campuses and, although this work has undoubtedly removed some of the difficulties that would otherwise have been encountered during the system merger exercise, they were not directly related to it, and are, therefore, outside the scope of this chapter.

Current automation and networking strategy

The automation and networking strategy which developed out of the historical and other factors detailed earlier, is described in this passage from a paper presented to the University during discussion about the possibility of purchasing a replacement system for the two libraries.

> The aims which will guide the Library's choice of a replacement system are set out below. These aims arise out of the Library's IT strategy, which is one element of General Library strategy and is an instrument of that strategy. The main value of automated systems, electronic forms of publication, and networks, is that they improve the efficiency of the Library by enabling it to effect the functions of information acquisition, provision, and communication with far greater speed and accuracy than could be achieved with traditional methods. The Geac and Dynix library housekeeping systems comprise only one element of IT utilization in the

Library, but it is an important one, and the procurement of a single system to replace them will play a key role in the development in the next stage of the Library's IT strategy. In choosing the replacement system, the Library's primary concern will be to ensure the maintenance of service improvements and efficiency levels already realised, whilst taking advantage of newer technologies with lower capital and maintenance costs. However, it will also seek to move towards the creation of a new kind of computing and networking environment appropriate to future requirements. It is envisaged that, a decade from now, computing and networking technologies will play an important role in the operational business of the University; that, in fact, a significant part of that business will take place through department-specific, campus-wide, national and international networks. This will require that the Library move towards a new kind of systems environment; one which draws together all of the various aspects of Library IT utilization into a single LAN-based environment in which systems are modular, distributed, integrated in the sense that modules are able to coexist and interwork, based on client/server architecture, and hospitable to emerging international networking and data description standards. In purchasing a replacement housekeeping system, therefore, the Library's secondary concern will be to begin to move towards this kind of environment.

The following statement of the Library's procurement aims is taken from its OR and gives an overview of the kind of system required.

Aims

In purchasing a replacement local library system, the Library's aims are:

- To replace both the Geac system installed at the John Anderson Campus and the Dynix system installed at Jordanhill campus with a single integrated system built around a single database and capable of serving the needs of both campuses whilst maintaining or improving upon the functionality of the present systems. It should be noted that maintaining the functionality of the present systems is a primary aim and takes precedence over all other aims. It is a minimum and mandatory requirement that the replacement system provide all functions and services specified as mandatory in the Operational Requirement.
- To replace the present software with software running on a range of non-proprietary hardware platforms under a UNIX System V Release 4 based operating system, in order to reduce dependence on a single hardware supplier, improve hardware reliability, and reduce recurrent costs (particularly hardware maintenance costs). If possible, the processing power will be divided between two machines, one at the John Anderson Campus, the other at Jordanhill Campus, the aim being to minimize downtime and protect services against the occurrence of a computer disaster at one or other site.
- To ensure, as far as possible, that all user services and facilities are fully available to all computer and network users on campus by installing a system that

will fully support access from a range of computers (e.g. IBM, Apple, Sun Workstations, VT100 terminals) and a range of network types (e.g. X.25, TCP/IP, Novell).

- To provide an improved service to users (more self-service functions, wider retrieval functions (e.g. searchable contents pages)), GUI-based manipulable outputs, extensions to networked services, e.g. online input of interlibrary loan requests and book purchase suggestions)
- To lay a sound and flexible foundation for future automation developments. In particular, by:

(a) Installing a system based on a client/server architecture distributed processing, a standard database management package, and modularized software, or, failing this, a system which provides a clear upgrade path towards a system of this type.

(b) Integrating user access to OPAC, local information sources such as CD-ROMs, and remote information sources (BIDS, WAIS, Gopher and so on) into a single workstation environment operable in roughly the same on a variety of GUIs.

(c) Integrating as many automated library functions into the associated Library LAN as possible. Many automated functions currently run on computers outwith the present central systems at the two campuses; the opportunity will be taken either to integrate these into the main system, or, more likely, into the extended Library network which will arise from its installation.

(d) Aiming to purchase a system which will, within a reasonable timescale, enable the provision of network and Library workstation access to full-text and multimedia publications as these become available.

- To enable import and export of data between the Library system and those of the Finance Office and Registry.
- To enhance the opportunities for future cooperation with other libraries and for the exploitation of services and facilities available over academic networks through a commitment to OSI standards.
- To improve management control of Library processes, through the provision of statistical and other reports, and the increased control of financial processes.
- To improve staff efficiency by providing desktop access to electronic mail; to networked printing, word-processing, and spreadsheet facilities; and to information services on the local CD network, on JANET (or SuperJANET), and on the Internet.

Selection of the new system

The case for replacement and the replacement schedule

A proposal to replace the Geac local library system (John Anderson Campus) and the Dynix local library system (Jordanhill Campus) with a single upgraded system by September 1995 was first put to the University in January 1994. The case for replacement was summarized as follows:

1 It will significantly reduce annual maintenance costs.
2 It will reduce the cost of on-going hardware purchases.
3 It will enable the library to maintain and improve staff efficiency.
4 A system of increased capacity will be required by 1995.
5 It will provide greatly improved facilities and an enhanced system design.
6 It is required to enable the completion of the harmonization of the library at Jordanhill campus with the main University Library.
7 It will enable the implementation of the next stage of the Library's IT strategy.

It is proposed that a replacement system be installed by September 1995. The Geac 9000 processor, which was installed in 1987, will be eight years old in 1995. Other parts of the Geac system, including six of the 340MB disk drives and many terminals are up to eighteen months older. The initial seven year maintenance contract is due to expire in November 1994 and a one year renewal will have to be requested to cover 1995. Hardware maintenance costs on the Geac system are now very high and it is expected that the purchase of a new system will be accompanied by a significant decrease in hardware maintenance costs. See appendix F [of the proposals] for details of present and estimated costs.

The Jordanhill Dynix System was purchased in 1989 and will therefore be due for replacement in 1996. However, it is already old technology compared to what is now available and response time problems are occurring at times of peak load. Both systems have software facilities which reflect the age of the hardware and which compare unfavourably with what is available from more modern systems.

The proposal then went on to indicate that the optimum time for the installation of the replacement system was May–September 1995. This would ensure that the effects of any attendant disruption to Library services and administrative processes would be minimized, and would also allow sufficient time for tendering under the EC procurement regulations.

At the same time, however, an earlier replacement date, May–September 1994, was also being considered. This was based on the so-called 'upgrade option'.

The upgrade option and the EC Procurement Regulations

The upgrade option and the EC Procurement Regulations were investigated in the first quarter of 1994. Since the University was aware that some other institutions had judged it permissable to 'replace' their present systems with an upgrade from their current suppliers rather than invite tenders under the EC Procurement Regulations, the option of doing this with one or other of the University's current suppliers was investigated, as were the Regulations themselves. The following is an edited version of the paper which considered the various options.

EC Procurement Regulations: four possible approaches

The EC Procurement Regulations recognise four possible approaches to a procurement. If the value of the procurement exceeds a certain threshold (2,000,000 ECUs, which is approximately £150,000), then one of the following must be applied:

> Open procedure
> Negotiated procedure
> Restricted procedure

If the value of the procurement is within this threshold then the buyer may proceed to purchase the goods required without reference to these procedures.

Dividing up procurements into constituent parts

It is acceptable to divide up procurements into constituent parts if there are sound procurement reasons for doing so. An example would be the purchase of microcomputers as system workstations. The University will almost certainly be able to purchase these at a lower price than the suppliers themselves could. It would therefore be perfectly reasonable to separate these out from the main procurement. It would not, however, be acceptable to split a procurement up into its constituent parts simply in order to circumvent the EC Regulations.

The upgrade option

The upgrade option may have the effect of bringing the replacement procurement below the threshold laid down in the EC Regulations. The basis of this is as follows:

1 The 160 microcomputers required as system workstations are separated from the main contract for procurement reasons (University can get a better price than suppliers).

2 The 50 printers required are similarly separated for the same reason.

3 Existing software licenses and hardware and software maintenance contracts with one of our current suppliers are extended. The total cost of these is certainly above the EC threshold but the view taken is that what is proposed within the upgrade option is an *extension* of an existing agreement *not* a new procurement, so that, arguably, the EC Regulations do not apply.

4 The central hardware is upgraded in year 1 at a capital cost within the EC procurement threshold.

5 If necessary, a further upgrade is purchased in year 3, again at a capital cost within the threshold.

The University must decide whether this position is a valid one. It is a position accepted by some within the University but rejected by others. Assuming it is a valid option, it has the following advantages:

- it reduces the effort and expenditure involved in replacing the Library's systems, since only two proposals must be evaluated
- it reduces the time required for choosing a system, thus allowing installation to start sooner
- it is alleged that it allows the companies concerned to reduce their costs and to pass these savings on to the customer (one company claimed that tendering usually costs a supplier around £40,000).

Taking the opposite view, however, it is possible to argue that an open tendering process is preferable because:

- it drives down costs by inviting wider competition
- it is impossible to be sure you have purchased the best system at the best price if you prejudge the issue by avoiding the open tendering process
- it is good procurement practice
- it is clearly within the EC Regulations and cannot be challenged later.

Open, restricted and negotiated procedures

Under the EC Regulations, procurements in excess of £150,000 must be handled through one of the following procedures:

- open
- restricted
- negotiated.

Further information on these procedures and when they may be applied is to be found in the attached extract from Statutory Instrument 1991 No. 2679, The Public Supply Contracts Regulations 1991.

The advantages and disadvantages held to be associated with the open procedure are listed earlier. The negotiated procedure does not apply to the circumstances of the present procurement (see 10(3)–10(8) of the Regulations). The restricted procedure might arguably be adopted on the grounds that only our present suppliers have the technical competence required to undertake a task which requires the conversion of both a Geac and a Dynix database into a single database (see 10(2)(b) and 12(14) of the Regulations).

Adoption of the restricted procedure in preference to the open procedure would have the advantage that it would probably reduce the number of tenders and so reduce the time and effort expended in the procurement process. It has the following disadvantages:

- unlike the open procedure, it may be challenged later and may have to be defended
- it reduces the level of competition.

In this particular circumstance, the restricted procedure has no significant advantage over the open procedure, since the selection criteria for the open procedure would include a requirement to prove technical experience of converting both Geac and Dynix systems and this would narrow the field just as effectively.

Conclusion
Only the upgrade option and the open procedure are worth considering further in the present circumstances.

In the event, the open tendering process was preferred over the upgrade option. The view taken was that this was both the safest and most sensible way forward. Unlike the open procedure, the upgrade option might have been open to challenge, particularly since neither Geac Advance nor Dynix Horizon would have been an upgrade in the strictest sense to a University running Geac 9000 and Dynix 'Classic' systems.

System size
One useful side effect of the investigation of the upgrade option was an agreement with the University regarding the size of the replacement system. The two existing suppliers had been asked to propose an upgrade based on the size of the current systems and on statistical projections and had come up with proposals for a 175 user system on the one hand and a 200 user system on the other. The following is a synopsis of the analysis the library put to the University.

A question obviously arises as to whether a 175 user system or a 200 user system is required. The present systems support 140 terminals, including network terminals at John Anderson campus. At John Anderson Campus, the present split between Library terminals and network terminals is 1 network terminal to every 4 Library terminals. Jordanhill Library has only just been put on the campus network. If the ratio of 1 to 4 applied there also, they require at this point in time 10 network terminals in addition to their 40 library terminals. On this basis, the present requirement is for a 150 user system.

However, this is based on a system to support a total of 20,000 users. In fact, it is estimated that a further 3000 users would be supported by 1995. Arguably, this would imply a 175 user system at minimum:

If 20,000 users require a 150 user system then 23,000 require an additional 150 x 3 = 23, so total requirement is approximately 175.

Further support for this as a minimum requirement comes from the fact that the Andersonian is expanding from a four to a five floor library. If four floors need 80 library terminals, five floors need an additional 20 terminals, taking the present requirement for 150 user system to a requirement for (again approximately) a 175 user system.

This is very much a minimum requirement. It does not take into account:

(a) A likely increase in network traffic over the next five years or so.
(b) Increases in throughput figures. For example, between 1984–5 and 1991–2, the number of borrowers increased from 10,715 to 13,138, but the

number of issues more than doubled, going from 252,972 to 564,488.

(c)   The possibility that the new system will encompass new modules – for example ILL.

In the event, the University decided that a 200 user system was required. If anything, subsequent usage levels have shown this to be an underestimate.

The selection process

During 1994, an OR for the replacement system was prepared by the Library Systems Division and subsequently accepted by the University's Library Computer Procurement Group (LCPG). An invitation to tender was placed in the *European journal* on 19 September 1994, indicating that a replacement system was sought. A set of evaluation criteria to be applied to the tenders was agreed by the LCPG, included in the invitation to tender and lodged with the Internal Audit office. These comprised 45 elements, subdivided into four general areas: software and design, hardware and performance, supplier assessment criteria and costs. Ten companies purchased the tender (priced at £100 to ensure that only serious enquiries were made). Five tenders were received by the closing date (18 November 1994).

The LCPG set up an Evaluation Subgroup to oversee the evaluation of the tenders, under the chairmanship of the Librarian. The Group included members of Library staff, the head of Management Information Services, the Procurement Officer and members of Computer Centre staff as required. Evaluation was carried out by the Library Systems Division with assistance and advice from other members of the Evaluation Subgroup.

Progress towards a final decision was made in three stages. An initial evaluation was carried out, looking in particular at mandatory requirements. At the end of this initial evaluation, two companies were agreed to have failed on mandatory requirements, and a shortlist of three companies was agreed by the Evaluation Subgroup. Two of these were regarded as clear front runners, with the third recognized as a weak third, with a particular weakness in the area of mandatory requirements relating to special loan and fine rules entailing conditionals. This company was asked to clarify whether or not they were offering special development to pass these mandatory requirements and they indicated that they were not. They were ruled out mainly because of this, but also because of a number of other shortcomings, i.e. they were a weak third for other reasons too.

The two remaining companies were looked at in exhaustive detail. A number of meetings were held with them in order to clarify aspects of their proposals. Demonstrations were arranged, reference sites were visited and their systems were closely examined against the evaluation criteria. It was finally agreed to recommend to the LCPG that, subject to clarification on a number of points, the Horizon system should be chosen and an order placed with Dynix. The other front runner was to be brought back into the reckoning if Dynix failed to satisfy the University on some final considerations.

Agreement was reached with Dynix and the company was presented with a letter of intent on 5 April 1995. This was followed by an official order on 7 April 1995. The other companies were then informed of the decision.

The Horizon system purchased by the University is based on client/server architecture, the Sybase RDBMS, and TCP/IP communications. All modules have GUI interfaces. The user OPAC client runs under MS Windows, X Windows or the Apple GUI (VT terminal access is also available). The various staff clients (circulation, cataloguing, book orders, serials, financial control, system administration and management information) run under OS/2 Warp, which is multitasking. The OPAC client and server software is Z39.50 compliant. Also included in the software package is the NetPublisher information service module. This is a combined Gopher, WWW and Z39.50 server and will enable the Library to enhance the service currently provided on WWW. The online catalogue has a facility which will allow electronic documents to be found through a catalogue search and automatically delivered to the desktop at the click of a mouse button. This has great potential for the future.

The system will support 200 simultaneous users within the guaranteed response times. This will notionally be made up of 160 physical IBM compatible microcomputers based in the various Library buildings (40 at Jordanhill) plus 40 'virtual' campus and/or Internet users. In practice, these numbers will vary depending on circumstances at any given time. Campus access will either be by Windows, X Windows or Apple GUI clients (probably available from the FTP server) or by VT terminal access. The system will be run on two servers, both HP G50 servers running UNIX. The main server is based in the Andersonian and supports all the main modules. A second server is based at Jordanhill. This acts as a VT terminal server and a Z39.50 server, but also offers OPAC back-up if the main system is down, management information functionality and disaster recovery back-up (required of the Library by the Internal Audit Office).

In the end, the choice between the two front runners was a difficult one, and the applicability of overall system design to the Library's automation and networking strategy was a significant factor in the decision. Amongst other things, the Library was looking for a system incorporating client/server architecture, distributed processing, a 'standard' database management package and modularized software, together with a range of other features which it believed would best enable it to implement its automation and networking strategy. It believed that a system of this type would be

- best suited to the present and future networking environment in the University
- most hospitable to the integration of other library IT facilities such as CD-ROM network access, client/server Internet access and Bath Information and Data Services (BIDS) access

- more flexible than other alternatives and, hence, more hospitable to future requirements
- more likely to be hospitable to a future in which the Library may prefer to 'mix and match' software modules from various suppliers so as to get the best available functionality across all modules
- more likely to be hospitable to a future gradual or phased replacement rather than complete replacement of the whole system at once.

It also believed that a system with these design features, by making more efficient use of the processing power and software resources of the microcomputers to be utilized as system workstations would be cheaper to purchase, maintain and extend or upgrade than other types of system. It was considered important that the Horizon system was designed as this type of system from the first.

Other significant factors taken into account in the final decision were

- an assessment of the stated preferences of key groups of Library staff regarding the three front runners.
- the fact that the Dynix Horizon system offered the preferred solution in terms of a combination of disaster recovery support, network response times management, OPAC back-up and Jordanhill response times protection, at a lower cost than the equivalent configuration from the alternative supplier (Dynix Horizon could be designed as a two processor system and, since it was a true client/server, the two processors required were less powerful than was the case in a two processor host-based system).

Installation of the new system

Progress towards the 'live' date

The installation effectively began in May 1995, the aim being to have the replacement system installed and running by 18 September 1995. This meant ensuring that all of the following operations were completed in good time.

Communications cabling

The whole of the main library and major parts of the Jordanhill library and satellite libraries had to be rewired with category 5 UTP ethernet cabling, this being the best that could be managed at the time and being susceptible to future upgrade when 100Mbits per second ethernet cards or ATM cards became reliably available. In order to allow response time guarantees to be tested in a fashion acceptable to both Dynix and the Library, two networks were to be installed in the main Library, one a user network, the other a staff network that could be closed off for the purposes of running a controlled test. Since the user network was also expected to be heavily used to access the CD-ROM network and a range of Internet services, this strategy also represented a useful way of protecting performance levels on the staff network, although this was only possible within the main Andersonian Library.

Implementation Largely completed on time. Most of the work on the installation of the two new library networks was completed by October, although a few lines remain to be tested, and one part of the level one 'patch panel' equipment is still not connected up. The original library ethernet was largely decommissioned by the end of October.

Purchase, delivery and installation of servers and associated peripherals and software

Two HP G50 servers were to be purchased, delivered to the Andersonian and Jordanhill libraries, installed with suitable software (UNIX, Sybase RDBMS, Horizon server software) and networked. Associated printers and scanners were also to be delivered. Client software was to be installed on two machines.

Implementation Completed on time (May 1995).

Purchase, delivery, installation and networking of microcomputers

One hundred and sixty PC compatible microcomputers, ranging from 75Mhz, 16MB RAM, 500MB disk machines to 90Mhz 32MB RAM, 500MB disk machines, were to be ordered, installed with OS/2 or Windows as appropriate, installed with appropriate TCP/IP software, networked and installed with Horizon software, Netscape, Telnet (part of TCP/IP) and Novell protocols for CD network access. Purchasing high specification PCs that would support client/server Horizon and multimedia Internet access, together with BIDS and Embase access and CD-ROM network access was a central part of the strategy – the idea being to form the basis for the electronic library of the future.

Implementation Completed on time.

System parameters agreed

It was necessary to agree on how system parameters would be set up well in advance of the live date.

Implementation Completed on time as far as was possible, given that some parts of the documentation were not comprehensive, follow up questions were often not answered and the set-up documentation related to an earlier version of the software.

Bibliographic data conversion mapping documents agreed

A specification of agreed mappings from the two existing bibliographic databases to the new, merged database had to be agreed with Dynix and sample data converted and tested.

Implementation Completed on time.

Integration of OCLC access with Horizon

Internet access to OCLC had to be installed on 11 machines at the two main sites and OCLC downloads integrated with the Horizon cataloguing module's import function.

Implementation Completed on time. By September, successful downloading of OCLC records to Horizon from OCLC was installed and working, together with appropriate field-mapping and item-mapping facilities.

Conversion of bibliographic data, creation of merged database, cataloguing live

Following the specification and the tests, the conversion itself had to take place, the merged database had to be put in place and cataloguing operations had to be switched from Geac and Dynix 'Classic' to Horizon.

Implementation Not completed on time. Many problems were encountered with this and only cataloguing of new records went live on 18 September 1995. Initial cataloguing was done onto a secondary database but copied to the primary database once the Geac bibliographic database had been converted and loaded. Cataloguing went 'live' at both sites on 18 September. The full database was not loaded for more than a month after the official live date, one of the main reasons why the whole project slipped.

Agreement on other data conversion requirements and special rules

Circulation data was to be converted and special loan and fine rules written and tested. Specifications for these had to be agreed before September if the live date was to be met.

Implementation Not completed on time. Throughout this quarter, intensive testing of special loan and fine rules written specifically for the Library was undertaken. Getting these right proved difficult. During September and October, work on the circulation conversion specification document was begun.

Acquisitions

For various reasons, the agreement with the company only allowed for the partial conversion of acquisitions data. The aim of this was to transfer an archive of acquisitions data to the Horizon server, so that it could be consulted. The possibility of limited receipting and invoicing facilities would also be investigated.

Implementation Not completed on time, but Dynix extended Geac maintenance to allow the job to be finished.

Training

Pre-install training was undertaken in June and systems training in July. Division staff organized their own training in respect of TCP/IP facilities, the OS/2 operating system and other related aspects of the new computing and networking environment. Training for the new system took place over August and September, covering all main modules. However, slippage in the implementation date meant that the timing of the training was less helpful than it might have been. Dynix did subsequently arrange various free 'top up' training sessions, however, and these have proved very useful.

Implementation   As described.

Interlibrary loans

Although loans were not due to become part of Dynix until later on in the project (we expect to beta test the software in 1997), urgent action was required during the installation process to convert the service to TCP/IP. This was necessary because the Computer Centre was removing X.25 access across the campus, one factor driving our change of networking strategy. A solution was found using a PICK to DOS conversion utility and an e-mail route to ARTtel.

Progress towards a stable working system: August 1995–August 1996

Towards the end of August 1995, Dynix announced both that Horizon release 4.0 containing reserve book room (short loan) and advance booking, user reservations and renewals, and the release the Library had actually ordered, would be delayed and that they would be unable to ensure 'live' running of the new system by the target date of 18 September 1995. It was agreed to go live with cataloguing only by this date and this was achieved. The next proposed date was 18 November 1995, the date on which Geac maintenance would cease. Since contractual negotiations were incomplete, it was agreed that Dynix should guarantee the continuance of the Geac maintenance in a separate letter. Confirmation of this was received during October. Although these delays were disappointing and disruptive, it is undoubtedly true that the target date of 18 September was extremely difficult to meet and that the Jordanhill element meant that, in effect, the company had two replacement installations and a merger on their hands, rather than one simple implementation.

In spite of all of the problems, however, system installation continued, moving slowly but surely towards a full live date. Conversion of the bibliographic database was completed by the end of October 1995 and cataloguing and public services went fully live soon after. Work on the specification for the circulation conversion then went ahead. A specification was agreed, test conversions were carried out for both of the old databases and circulation finally went live in late December 1995 in the Andersonian, Law, Fleck and Business Libraries and in January 1996 at Jordanhill. Acquisitions, serials and financial control went live soon after, although this was a slow, largely manual process. The partial conversion of the Geac acquisitions records for archiving purposes continued after this date and was not completed until March 1996

Unsurprisingly, perhaps, going live with Horizon was not the end of our problems. There were at least three reasons for this. First, we went live with version 3.2 of the software, as opposed to 4.0, a factor which ensured not only a significant downgrade in functionality in many areas (e.g. loss of reserve book room at the Andersonian and self-service functions – self-reservations, self-renewals and advance booking – at Jordanhill), but also having to work with a number of features regarded as 'odd' by staff on the main campus (e.g. renewals calculated from the previous due date and expiry dates calculated as a number of days after registration, a feature that has been made optional since). Second, the 3.2 software proved to have a number of 'bugs' which took time to sort out and left a degree of disruption in their wake. Third, there were, despite very careful testing of the demonstration conversions, significant problems with the converted data, both in circulation and in the bibliographic database. The problems with the latter were particularly disruptive to library users, and were exacerbated by system parameterization problems, resulting in a number of public access catalogue (PAC) indexing and display peculiarities (e.g. the so-called 'd' problem (now fixed), which meant that in order to retrieve words containing 'd' in certain indexes you had to omit the 'd', so 'indian' became 'inian').

As if these problems were not enough, a new shortcoming of the system came to light during this period, particularly prominent in the acquisitions area. It became clear not only that version 3.2 of the software did not contain many of the promised features, but that the next upgrade, now to be called 4.1, would not contain them either. Indeed, on investigation, it became clear that it was probably too late to get these features into 4.2 and we would have to wait until 4.3 before they arrived. On discovering this problem, a trawl through the OR and the company's tender and accompanying letters of clarification was made and all problem areas were identified. New agreements were then reached with the company entailing extended implementation dates, compensation of various kinds in respect of the Library, and – crucially – an agreed programme of works over the summer of 1996 aimed at fixing the databases, upgrading the software and aiming to ensure a more stable environment for staff and users in the 1996–7 academic year.

The summer programme – carried out by a new Project Manager, who had a library systems background – was recognized by systems staff as a watershed. Significant improvements were essential by the beginning of the new academic year, notwithstanding the fact that systems staff, generally speaking, felt that the major part of the job had been successfully completed. The suggestion made by some library staff that a move to an alternative system be considered was not seen as a serious possibility, in that it would

- only become an option once the conversion problems were sorted out
- even then, be a dubious way forward, partly because there was no guarantee that switching to a new company at that stage would not cause a further period of difficulty, partly because it was felt that, despite the problems, the right choice of system had been made in the first place.

The importance of the summer programme was made clear to Dynix and they delivered on the most crucial factors, although library staff also made significant contributions to its success.

The summer programme

Over the summer and into October 1996, a significant programme of work was undertaken, aimed at cleaning up the database, improving indexing facilities, extending user services and other functionality, and at moving forward those elements of the implementation of the system still outstanding (a process now expected to extend until the end of 1997). A number of problems with existing indexes were fixed during this period and most indexes are now operating correctly. New indexes were added, e.g. an improved class number index and a Special Collections index. UDC filing is still a problem but we are told that version 4.2 is the answer.

During July 1996, the system software was upgraded to version 4.1, bringing improved functionality in a number of areas, particularly circulation. New facilities for users were also introduced. PAC renewals are now available on both campuses and so also are self-renewals. In addition, library electronic services began to be delivered to users via the online catalogue, user workstations began offering access to electronic services like BIDS, the CD network, other library catalogues via WWW, and Internet services such as BUBL, EEVL, and NISS when the PAC went live in late 1995. However, access is now effected via the catalogue, with users searching in the catalogue for the service they want, then clicking a 'hot spot' on the screen to access the electronic service they are interested in, which is then delivered to the desktop. This is seen as a prelude to imposing access control on some or all of these services in order to meet new University regulations, and as a partial implementation of the results of the CATRIONA Project.[1]

Other developments over this period included the running of year end procedures for the first time in financial control, the loading of registration data for the first time from data files supplied by registry, progress with Z39.50 implementation and the implementation of an improved library WWW service, using the Dynix NetPublisher software. The improvements hoped for in the alternative telnet-based text-only version of the networked catalogue have not yet materialized. However, Dynix have agreed to implement this improvement during the next stages of the schedule. They have offered Lynx access to their WebPAC product as an alternative to the current product and have stated that this should give us all of the functionality previously promised. An additional benefit which will arise from this development is that access to the catalogue through WWW clients such as Netscape will become possible.

The good news is that, although there are still considerable amounts of work to be done and areas of functionality still to be delivered, the system now seems to have stabilized and is providing a good service in some areas (cataloguing, and user services), a satisfactory service in serials control, an adequate service with room for improvement in circulation and a basic service in the remaining area of acquisitions (in which much of the functionality not now due till the end of 1997 is concentrated). Reserve book room will not be implemented in the main library until the first quarter of 1997 and it will be a mainly manual process. Discussions are still on-going regarding the implementation of advance booking. On the positive side, the bedrock of our new automation and networking strategy is now in place, the system at the heart of it is now functioning reasonably well and we can look towards the future with a degree of optimism.

At the time of writing – October 1996 – the basic system is largely in place, but a number of issues are outstanding. These are expected to be dealt with by the end of 1997 and relate partly to undelivered functionality, partly to on-going installations. The major items are

- replacement of current telnet (i.e. non-GUI) network access with WebPAC and Lynx (requires Sybase upgrade and Horizon 4.2)
- completion of Z39.50 implementation (requires Horizon 4.2 and some further implementation work)
- installation of second server as a disaster recovery, OPAC back-up and management information service
- reserve book room to go live at Anderson Campus (Library responsibility)
- advance booking to go live at both campuses
- installation of second self-issue system in the Law Library
- outstanding acquisitions enhancements (requires Horizon 4.3, or 5.1, as the Windows 95 version will be called)
- interlibrary loans (not yet released)
- stock control (requires Library specification)
- OS/2 to Windows 95 change.

Staff-related issues

In retrospect, it is clear that more could have been done locally to help staff through the difficulties that arose due to the various problems that were encountered during the introduction of Horizon. Unfortunately, we did not foresee the level of disruption that would ensue. Had we done so, systems staff might have considered asking that a relatively senior member of professional staff be assigned to help address staff concerns and act as liaison between systems staff and other staff on an on-going basis until at least October 1996. In the event, systems staff themselves attempted to undertake this task, but spent too much time 'firefighting' and managing the implementation itself and its problems to address staff concerns adequately or devote enough time to it. An attempt was made for a time to have regular 'systems surgeries', but these ceased as the workload and pressure on systems staff (and, indeed, other staff) increased. A member of non-systems staff devoted to this purpose might have taken some of the pressure from systems and other staff alike. Given the present staffing situation, it might well have proved difficult or even impossible to assign someone to this task, but it is certainly something we would consider in future – and would recommend that other libraries consider seriously. The member of staff would have to be chosen with great care, of course. Even when an implementation goes smoothly, it is a task requiring tact, diplomacy, empathy with staff problems in all areas (including, of course, systems) and an understanding of the issues involved, the requirement that proceeding with the implementation be a paramount consideration and the aims of the organization in respect of the new environment that is being created. If things do not go smoothly, the person concerned has the unenviable task of liaising between two groups of equally overworked and pressured staff. But the potential benefits to all concerned are great and it is certainly an idea worthy of serious consideration. Moreover, if someone else does not handle these problems, the systems team has to do it, and they already have more than enough on their hands during a major system replacement exercise, especially if all is not going according to plan.

At this point in time, very little consideration has been given to other staffing issues which might arise as the result of the installation of a new system. Although no major structural changes are currently envisaged, it may be that some may suggest themselves as time goes on. Some new roles may also emerge. At this stage, however, this is entirely speculative. Some changes in working practices have been forced on staff due to missing functionality, particularly in the acquisitions area, but it is not yet clear whether these will be temporary or permanent. Changes in working practices were not a planned part of the replacement exercise and will only be undertaken where they are either sensible or necessary.

Training

Until the advent of the summer programme, training was generally inadequate to the task of preparing the staff for dealing with the problems they faced. The reasons for this include:

- sometimes the Dynix staff were so new to the system that they were, almost literally, only a few pages of the manual ahead of library staff
- often the training was done on schedule but the system module it covered was implemented several months late, bringing the need for top up training which, although, generally speaking, delivered, was often much later than we would have liked and, in any case, sometimes suffered from the first reason given
- training staff were seldom sufficiently *au fait* with the system to tailor the training to Strathclyde's specific requirements
- training staff often did not have sufficient knowledge of libraries or, if they did, of the library area covered by the module they were presenting (questions like 'What exactly is a standing order?' were encountered all too frequently).

The problem with the early training may have been due to a combination of our unique training requirements, a lack of knowledge and understanding of the application and an imbalance between the technical and library-level input at the supplier end. The latter factor, in particular, may have led to an overly technical approach resulting in trainers who were poorly briefed about our working practices.

This raises the question of whether a technical approach to the project was what we required. A more desirable approach would have been to have a library consultant with experience of library systems and library practices assigned, together with a technical resource to our project.

Training improved significantly during the summer programme, mainly due to the new Project Manager who had a library background in systems and acquisitions and understood our needs without much assistance from us. A series of (free) 'consultancy days' were organized which covered various system modules and attempted to be specific to our own local implementation. We were also offered a free systems training course, which improved our understanding greatly. Another reason for the improved performance as regards training was that the Dynix staff had learned a great deal about the system in their attempts to sort out the problems at Strathclyde and at the other UK Horizon sites.

Conclusions

There is good reason to suppose that by the end of 1997 all of the main aims of the procurement will have been met. All of the major problems have been overcome and it should now only be a question of time. Given that meeting these aims was not only a worthwhile objective but also a necessary one, the question of whether or not it was wise to choose a relatively untried system, especially in view of the tight timescale, translates into a question of whether or not these aims might have been met in the same or, at least, an acceptable timescale, but with less pain and disruption, by another route. Since waiting until 1997 to reduce maintenance bills and upgrade ageing and ailing systems was not an option, this, in turn, translates into a question of whether or not the aims might have been met in the same or a similar timescale but with less disruption had another system been chosen.

It is not possible to know the answer to this question for certain, because there is no way of knowing the level of pain and disruption that might have been suffered (or spared) if another system had been chosen. The best we can say is that, first, of the systems on offer, there was only one other option that might have allowed us to meet all of our aims in the same or, at least, an acceptable timescale. Aside from this one and Dynix Horizon itself, all of the other suppliers who bid were unsuitable for one reason or another. Those felt to be generally acceptable in terms of system design and our aims, were considered to be too underdeveloped. The others, who ruled themselves out on other grounds (e.g. cost and failure to meet mandatory requirements), in any case were felt to be unacceptably proprietary (in system design terms), and would have left us facing, in five, six or seven years time, the same problems it faced this time around. Only one other of those on offer had at least the potential of meeting all of our aims in a similar timescale.

Second, we made our choice between the two systems on the shortlist on a sound basis, the preferred system being chosen on the grounds detailed earlier, including:

- the fact that the system concerned had been designed from the first as the kind of system we were looking for, whereas the alternative was, it was claimed, being developed into this kind of system gradually (one question asked was whether it was really possible to do this and, hence, whether this company could really meet our aims at the time in question)
- a lower cost, apparently attributable in the main to the fact that Horizon had been developed from the first as the kind of system we were looking for.

Third, whilst we clearly cannot say without a shadow of a doubt that we could not have met our aims in the same or, at least, an acceptable timescale, but with reduced pain and disruption if we had chosen another supplier, we can say that

- we have no evidence to suggest that choosing the alternative would necessarily have been either a trouble-free or a delay-free option
- on current evidence we will meet all our aims, particularly those relating to system and network design, earlier by our chosen route than we would have done via our one alternative route
- at the time of writing, the question of whether or not the alternative option really can be developed into the kind of system we wanted remains unanswered.

In short, the closest we can come to answering the question as to whether or not we made the right choice is to say

- there is no particularly strong evidence to suggest that we might have avoided the pain and disruption in what was, after all, an extremely complex replacement project, by choosing an alternative system
- there is comfort in the fact that, on the one hand, it now looks reasonable to believe that we will have achieved all of our major aims by the end of 1997 and, on the other, that we have no conclusive evidence as yet to show that we would have been in the same or a similar position by then had we opted for our one real alternative
- that our aims were worth meeting and we can now look forward to building the systems and services that staff and users require and deserve.

This answer may not satisfy everyone, but it is the kind of answer that most systems librarians have learnt to live with and it will have to suffice.

Reference

1 Nicholson, D. et al., *Cataloguing the Internet: CATRIONA feasibility study*, London, British Library, 1995 (LIR report; 105).

A double migration at San Joaquin Valley Library System – the systems vendor's perspective

Mark Evans

Introduction

This is a case study of a system migration performed by Ameritech Library Services. At the time this migration was done, the name of the company was Dynix Inc., and it will be referred to here as 'Dynix'.

Dynix is experienced in migrating data from a number of other library automation systems. System migrations constitute 30–50% of Dynix customers that are in the installation process at any one time. With this amount of migrations it is necessary for Dynix to maintain a team of personnel who are well-trained in migrating systems. Dynix personnel had previously performed migrations from the vendors used in the following case study, and, as a result, methodology and procedures had been fine-tuned.

This case study will explore the migration of the San Joaquin Valley Library System (SJVLS), located in the San Joaquin Valley area of the state of California in the USA. SJVLS was the result of a merger of two previously autonomous library systems: Fresno and Bakersfield. These two library systems together comprised 107 branch libraries spread over a seven county area. Each county had its own cataloguing centre where materials for that county were ordered, received, catalogued and distributed to the various branches within that county. Once merged, their combined database would contain over 630,000 bibliographic records, 3,000,000 individual items, 600,000 patrons and an annual circulation of over 5,000,000. This case study describes the flow of the migration, but does omit explanations of certain data structures and procedures as they are proprietary to Dynix and to other library automation vendors.

Before the merger into SJVLS, Fresno and Bakersfield were independent political entities. They each had their own sources of funding, staff hierarchy and procedures. The decision to merge into a single entity would cause some restructuring of procedures, but would result in an entity better able to meet the needs of its patrons.

Prelude to migration

At the time of migration, Fresno was using a Ulisys system. Bakersfield was using an LS2 system. Since Fresno and Bakersfield were on different library automation systems, two separate migrations would need to be performed. It was decided that although two migrations would be performed, all consultation and meetings would include both Fresno and Bakersfield personnel. To this end, a committee was formed from Fresno and Bakersfield staff to address the questions of the consortium at large. Any questions that dealt with only one of the systems would be answered by staff from that system.

The two main considerations of a system migration are the quality of the data transfer, followed closely by how much time the library will be without an automated system. Even the smallest libraries that utilize automation systems view downtime with distaste. Patrons who are used to quick checkout or rapid access to system information are displeased with the sketchiness or complete lack of facilities during a system migration. The shine of exceptional quality data can be tarnished by a long period of migration where the library will not be able to provide service to its patrons. Conversely, a shoddy job of transferring data will offset the gains made by a speedy migration.

After the contract to purchase the Dynix system was signed, a group from SJVLS travelled to Dynix headquarters in Provo, Utah, for a pre-installation meeting. This meeting was held in Provo so that the SJVLS staff could meet all the people who would work on their migration and see the company structure and workings at first-hand. This pre-installation meeting was held early on in the implementation phase, some weeks before the installation was to begin, so that problems could be identified and solved before they affected the libraries' functions during the migration. Topics covered in this meeting were

- a review of contract
- the identification and definition of system software parameters
- maintenance
- a review of hardware and telecommunications to be installed
- a review of migration procedures.

One of the topics covered in the pre-installation meeting that directly impacted the schedule of the migration was the hardware and telecommunications installation. SJVLS purchased their main computer system and telecommunications equipment through Dynix. This was preferred as this put the onus of keeping to the installation schedule under one entity rather than two. Coordination between one company, which installs hardware, and a second company, which installs software, can become tricky and sometimes tangled. Failure to communicate can cause delays in the implementation of a system. Involving two separate companies increases the likelihood of misunderstandings. In the case of SJVLS, the sheer scope of the system implementation called for some tight timing to get the system up and operational as rapidly as possible. There was no room for communication failure. This pressure was eased somewhat as Dynix controlled both the hardware and software installs. The person performing the data migration and the person responsible for the hardware installation formed a cohesive team that was able to coordinate the various pieces quickly. SJVLS also purchased new terminals through Dynix. Since few librarians want two different terminals (old vendor's and Dynix) cluttering up their desks, it was possible to coordinate migration activities so that the new terminals would be installed shortly before the data migration was completed.

The identification and definition of system software parameters was also an important part of the pre-installation visit. Although there are general similarities among the many library automation system vendors (they all check items in, check them out and catalogue them), the flow and ways in which these tasks are accomplished differ widely. The person assisting SJVLS in setting up their system parameters needed to understand how the libraries currently functioned, and how they wanted to function after merging into one library system. Once Dynix personnel understood the current workflow and desired alterations of SJVLS, they were able to relate it to how the Dynix product functions and how the parameters needed to be set up to best accommodate the libraries. Even under the best of circumstances, no library automation system can be expected to perform exactly like another. During a migration, a library can expect to make certain small alterations to its workflow to make the most efficient use of its new library automation system. The job of the automation vendor is to make these workflow alterations as small as possible. Faced with a new system, library staff cannot be expected to etch their system parameter decisions into stone immediately. There is always some parameter fine-tuning that must be done once a system is operational and the library has a chance for all of its staff to exercise the system. The goal at the pre-installation meeting with SJVLS was to understand workflow and to hammer out a set of parameters that would cover the majority of the system's workflow.

Once the library obtained a general idea of their system parameters, it was time to discuss the migration of data from the old library automation system to the new one. The goal was to migrate the data as quickly and cleanly as possible. There is always a trade-off between time and cleanliness. No matter how careful the library automation package or vigilant the library staff, data corruption will occur on any system. The correct authority may not be associated with a particular bibliographic record, a patron's address may be mangled or an item may be checked out to two different patrons at the same time. The library staff must understand the credo of GIGO: Garbage In, Garbage Out. The cleanliness of the migration depends on the quality of data coming from the old automation system. Anything can be perfected if enough time and resources are dedicated to it. However, time is of the essence in a system migration. A library must understand up front that if bad data is extracted from the old machine, time spent cleaning it up could keep the new library automation system from coming up live. Any data clean-up that the library can perform before the migration begins can impact the speed of the migration. Examples of data clean-up that the library can do are to delete unwanted bibliographic records from its system and to clean up patron information that is known to be corrupted. Dynix has found that 3–5% of a library's records can be corrupted.

Dynix has found that a migration can be performed in stages. Each stage consists of moving a particular segment of the library's data from the old system to the new system. In this way, only one aspect of the library's functions are affected, thus decreasing the annoyance to staff and patrons. The stages used in the migration of the SJVLS data were

1 bibliographic data (in the form of MARC records), including individual items
2 patron data
3 circulation information
4 blocks on patron borrowing privileges
5 holds.

Each segment of data was extracted from the old system and processed into the new system without the other segments being affected. This also eased the pressure on the installation of telecommunications equipment. No matter how efficiently it is done, it takes time to install hundreds of terminals spread out over 107 branches. When one data segment is being migrated, efforts can be concentrated to install workstations in that one area of operations. In the case of SJVLS, there were seven different cataloguing centres. While the migration of the bibliographic data was going on, the terminals and telecommunications hardware could be going in at those seven sites. Once a particular segment of data was migrated to the new machine, library staff could start using the new library automation system with that data while the next segment was being migrated.

This processing of separate segments also allowed a cleaner migration. When a particular segment is migrated, the library staff reviews it for accuracy. Any problems with the migration of that data segment can be corrected easily. In addition, some data clean-up of 'garbage' data from the old system can be done if time allows. Note that each segment of data builds on the segment before it. For example, the basis for all operations of a library automation system is the bibliographic data of the material in the library. If that is migrated badly and data verification is delayed until the end of the migration, clean-up will be much more complicated.

No matter how many migrations of a particular type have been performed by a library automation vendor, it is important to obtain samples of data. Different releases of any one vendor's system may contain slightly different data structures. Although a library does not intentionally mislead a vendor, sometimes the data definitions and content of records actually in a database may differ from what the library says. Dynix has found that a good random sample of 10–15% of the records in a database should provide a sufficient basis to plan a migration.

One of the tedious, but vital, portions of the migration preliminaries is the translation of coded values. Every prominent library vendor uses coded fields to some extent. A coded field will contain a particular character string that will represent the same value across many records, and guarantees data consistency.

An example of a coded field would be a city code. The city of 'San Francisco' can be misentered by library staff, with the database ending up containing cities like 'San Fancisco', 'San Franisco', 'San Franciso', etc. If a city field contains the code of 'SF', then 'SF' can be defined by the system to mean exactly 'San Francisco' and nothing else. The way the various library automation vendors utilize codes differs. It is rarely possible to transfer codes from one system to another and have them mean exactly the same thing. The functionality of one code on a particular system may need to be divided into two different codes on another system, or vice-versa. Part of the pre-installation meeting is to go over the record format from the old system with the library staff, determine which fields are coded fields, and how to map those codes to the Dynix system. It is imperative that the library present a complete list of codes on the old system and what they are to be on the Dynix system before the migration even begins so that data verification and clean-up can proceed as quickly as possible.

A question that burns on the lips of libraries about to undergo a system migration is 'How long will it take?'. This is a tricky question to answer. Much depends on the computer hardware. Since the systems that Fresno and Bakersfield were using had older hardware, the extraction of information was a big time factor. No matter what system a library is using, if they are switching to another vendor, it is almost a certainty that their previous hardware is older, slower technology. SJVLS purchased a Sequoia computer. The Sequoia was designed to be a multi-user, fault-tolerant system. The tape and disk drive controllers were intelligent, taking some responsibility off the shoulders of the central processing unit (CPU) and increasing the processing power of the computer. The Sequoia also had two tape drives and multiple processors so data could be loaded at a faster rate. Data samples are invaluable in giving the length of time necessary for the migration as a test can be made with real data. Every vendor does benchmarks with their product on various hardware platforms, and Dynix is no different. However, benchmarks and real situations can differ greatly. During the pre-installation visit with SJVLS, a preliminary schedule was created. Fresno was to be migrated first, followed after a brief time by Bakersfield. This allowed the library to make sure that one migration was clean before commencing on the second. The total time from beginning of hardware installation through the completion of the second migration was 13 weeks. This may seem like a long time, but remember that this included two migrations and a lull between migrations of eight weeks for Bakersfield to prepare their staff and physical facilities. The SJVLS staff were quite content with the schedule outlined.

Different library automation system vendors sometimes use different terms for the same data or procedure. Terms can also differ from country to country. A 'checkout' in one automation system may mean the same thing as 'charge' in another. 'Request', 'hold' or 'reservation' may also mean the same thing among different systems. It is important to clarify with the customer what exactly is meant by any particular term. In the case of SJVLS, both previous automation systems used different terminology. It has been found by Dynix that customers can readily and rapidly pick up the terminology used in the Dynix system, so this period of transition is not very long, although the migration personnel must be aware of the customer's old terminology. SJVLS proved to be among the fastest to adapt to the new Dynix terminology.

Bibliographic migration

As stated earlier, Fresno was the first of the two library systems to migrate to Dynix. The migration of the bibliographic data commenced on 13 August. Migrating bibliographic data is the easiest part of the entire process. MARC records have become the standard form for transferring and storing biblio-graphic information. The Ulisys system that Fresno previously used had the capability to output MARC records to half-inch tape reels. The Ulisys system had the added benefit of putting item information into the MARC record.

Before Fresno began to extract the bibliographic data from their Ulisys sys-tem, all cataloguing was stopped. This was done so that no new records or mod-ifications to existing records would be missed by the extraction. Other functions of the library, public access and circulation, continued as normal because these functions do not modify the content of bibliographic records. Although there was no automated system for the cataloguers to use, this did not mean that they were idle. There were other tasks that needed to be done by hand that could be done at this time (e.g. unpacking new shipments, making sure that previously catalogued material was distributed to the proper site and practising on the new Dynix software using a training database). During this time, the new terminals and telecommunication equipment were installed for the cataloguing staff.

Once the bibliographic data was migrated to the new Dynix system, the cat-aloguing staff connected to the Dynix system and verified the proper transfer of data. A few Ulisys terminals had been left in the various cataloguing offices so that checks could be made against the old system to see if a problem was caused by the migration, or if it was bad data to begin with.

Once the bibliographic data was pronounced good by the Fresno cataloguing staff, item creation was executed. Information to create item records came from the 949 tag in the MARC record. A sample of items was created from various MARC records so that library staff could quickly verify that the items were being created in the way they wanted. Verification of coded fields was also done at this time. Libraries have been known to change their minds about coded fields from the time the system parameters are drawn up to the time they give a list of code translations to the Dynix personnel performing the migration. SJVLS was no exception. Certain codes were spelled differently, others were changed totally. However, the case of SJVLS was clean, as few of the codes changed from parameter setting to migration. Once the library indicated that the items were being created in accordance with the specifications, items were created for the rest of the MARC records. When the item creation finished, the cataloguing staff could resume their daily work using the new Dynix system.

Patron information migration

Once the migration of the bibliographic MARC data from Ulisys to Dynix had been completed, but before the item creation was done, the migration of the patron information was initiated. This was done to narrow the window of the migration as much as possible. As stated earlier, the hardware of the Ulisys system was older, slower technology. By the time the patron data was extracted, and processing onto the new Dynix system had begun, the item creation would be finished.

While patron information was being extracted from the Ulisys system and loaded into the Dynix system, the circulation staff had to stop registering new patrons on the Ulisys system. This did not mean that they turned new patrons away. Since Fresno required new patrons to fill out a paper form anyway, library cards were still issued to new patrons and the paper forms kept in a safe place to be entered later into the Dynix system. Other circulation functions continued as normal: checking material in and out, placing holds and public access.

When the patron information was extracted from the Ulisys system, a small sample was processed for the library to verify that it was being done in accordance with the specifications. When the sample was approved, the entire patron base was loaded into the Dynix system. Once the processing of the entire patron base had been completed, the library once again reviewed the data. Coded fields were also verified to make sure that no code had been missed.

The entire process of transferring patron information took three days, including extraction, loading and verifying. When the library certified that the patron data had been migrated according to the specifications, the library staff entered into the Dynix system all the patron forms gathered in the period during which automated patron registration was unavailable.

Circulation migration

The circulation information actually consisted of three separate pieces: item status (out, in, lost, etc.), fines and holds. These three pieces were migrated as one because they are the most volatile of library information. While bibliographic and patron data change, they do not do so at a rate as fast as the circulation data. Also, the circulation desk is the most visible part of the library, and any problems there are quite noticeable to the patrons. In the case of both Fresno and Bakersfield, local taxes account for a good portion of the library revenue, so they wanted to keep the patrons as pleased about the system migration as possible.

The migration of circulation information did not start until the bibliographic, item and patron information was completely migrated to the Dynix system, and the library had verified that the data was accurate and clean. The migration of circulation data also depended on each branch using the new terminal and telecommunications equipment to access the Dynix system. It is a good idea to arrange the migration of circulation data over a weekend, holiday or other time when the branches are closed, so that it affects the patrons as little as possible.

Once the circulation data was on the Dynix system, the library staff reviewed it for accuracy. Again, a few terminals were left connected to the Ulisys system for checking on any problems that may have occurred. Once the circulation data was migrated and verified, the circulation staff could come up live on the Dynix system.

Completion of Fresno

The migration was declared complete by library staff on 30 August, taking 17 days from start to finish. The things that affected the time schedule the most were

- extraction of data from the previous Ulisys system
- data verification.

It was some time after the migration was completed before public access terminals were activated. One reason for this was that the number of public access terminals was much greater in relation to the number of staff (both cataloguing and circulation), and it took longer to install all the new Dynix terminals. Another reason was that the library staff wanted to make sure that the public searches were set up and operating in the way that most patrons could easily understand and use.

As is the case with almost every migration, no matter how carefully the library staff verifies the migrated data, problems appear later on. Dynix did minor data clean-up projects for several weeks after the migration was declared completed by the library. These minor points of clean-up mainly dealt with problems caused by the migration rather than data from the Ulisys system.

Migration of Bakersfield

The migration of the LS2 system utilized by Bakersfield followed the same scheme as that of Fresno. It goes without saying that different extraction and loading programs were used as Fresno was on a different automated system.

The migration began on 27 October. The extraction of the MARC data from the LS2 system and loading it into the Dynix system took seven days. The extraction and loading of the patron data took three days. The circulation data required four days to extract and load, whereas the block and hold information required only one day. The migration was completed on 11 November, a total of 16 days. This time, the item that caused the biggest time delay was distance. The LS2 computer was located in Bakersfield, but the computer that Dynix installed was located in Fresno, over 106 miles away. Each time a tape of data was extracted from the LS2 system, it had to be sent via courier to the computer centre in Fresno. This almost always took an entire day, with an occasional delay of two days due to a weekend.

It should be pointed out at this point that no elimination of duplicate records was done during the migration from the LS2 to Dynix. Fresno and Bakersfield shared many bibliographic records, as well as some patron records. It was decided to have duplicate records on the system for the short period of the migration as it reduced potential problems of attaching item and circulation information. The process of removing duplicate records will be discussed later.

The most visible problem after the migration of the Bakersfield LS2 system was 'ghost' barcodes. The Dynix system has the capability of letting the user enter just the significant portions of a barcode and the Dynix system will append the appropriate beginning characters and any institution code being used. Once the barcode is made complete, a check digit algorithm is used to verify correct entry of the barcode. The problem arose because although both Fresno and Bakersfield used two different barcode types and two different check digit algorithms, it was possible for a barcode from one system to be made valid for the other. An example would be the barcode R0000010689. If a circulation clerk in Bakersfield entered just the significant digits of 10689, the Dynix system would use the Bakersfield algorithm and flesh out the barcode to be R0000010689. The Bakersfield check digit algorithm would verify that indeed this was a valid barcode. However, if a circulation clerk in Fresno entered the significant digits 10689, the Dynix system would use the Fresno algorithm to flesh out the barcode to be 33109000010689 and the Fresno check digit algorithm would verify that this was a valid barcode. Once the two systems merged, they began to exchange material more freely. A circulation clerk might enter just the significant digits of a barcode and be told that while it was a valid barcode format, it did not exist in the database, because the wrong algorithm was being use to construct the complete barcode and verify the check digit. Or, a circulation clerk might enter the significant digits of a barcode, the Dynix system would use the wrong algorithm to complete and verify the barcode, and check the wrong item to the wrong patron.

This was corrected by modification of the barcode algorithms and education of the circulation staff. The barcode algorithms were adjusted, so if a barcode was fleshed out, but it didn't exist in the database, then the other barcode algorithm was used to see if it completed a barcode that did exist on the system. This corrected the majority of the problems. Educating the circulation clerks to notice the other style of barcodes and to consciously double-check how the system fleshed out the barcode resolved the rest of the problems. Granted, these problems were relatively few in number, but they occurred just often enough to be bothersome to patrons and staff.

Elimination of duplicate records

Once both migrations were complete and all library staff were comfortable with the data, it was time to remove duplicate records from the system. The SJVLS staff decided that since the number of patrons having both Fresno and

Bakersfield library cards was quite small, they would deal with these on an individual basis as the library cards expired. The bibliographic data was somewhat more difficult to 'de-duplicate'.

Duplicate records did not account for a large portion of the entire SJVLS collection, but it was enough to cause patrons some consternation when they saw two items in public access and they did not know which one to look at. Many of the duplicate records contained control numbers such as OCLC or LC that could be used to match. In the case of Fresno and Bakersfield having duplicate bibliographic records, it was decided to use Bakersfield's copy. A process was executed that went through the database, matching records based on the control numbers, determining which bibliographic record to keep, then merging all the items and holds from the duplicate records to the one record being kept. The duplicate record or records were deleted.

This process did not take care of all the duplicates. As was stated earlier, no matter how careful the library staff is, some discrepancies in the data will creep into the system. There were many duplicate records that did not contain common control numbers. The only way to tell that they were duplicate records was by examining the title, author and publication data. After conferring with SJVLS staff, it was decided to use a normalized form of the title, author and publication information as match points for duplicate records. It was also decided not to have the computer do the matching and removing of duplicate records automatically using this method. Sometimes a portion of the information used to determine a normalized match point was missing from records, and although they were truly not duplicates, the match criteria said that they were. A program was written especially for SJVLS so that they could examine the list of possible duplicates that the computer produced, and decide on a case-by-case basis if the records were really duplicates to be merged or just superficially similar. This method required more staff time than an automatic merger, but it guaranteed more accurate results.

Conclusions

The migration of the SJVLS was one of the largest and most complex migrations that Dynix (now known as Ameritech Library Services) has performed. It was chosen for this case study as it provides examples of situations not normally encountered in the migration of smaller systems. Migrations of large systems create problems that are different from migrations of smaller systems, both in logistics and timing. Problems encountered by merging two systems into one – basically performing two individual migrations – also provided some interesting views of library migrations.

Migrations, independent of automation vendors, generally follow the same formats. Procedures used by the Dynix UK office do not differ greatly from those used by Dynix USA. This case study, therefore, holds validity independent of geographical location.

The greatest factors that govern how smoothly and quickly a migration is done are the library staff and the computer hardware involved. The library staff will provide sample data, decide on system parameters and verify whether data is migrated correctly. A professional staff will accomplish all of these tasks in a timely manner. The staff at SJVLS excelled at providing answers on time, and cooperating with Dynix migration staff. The computer hardware will determine the rate at which data is loaded and processed. The Sequoia at SJVLS provided consistent, error-free performance. Both these factors combined to make the library migration a success.

5 Automation and migration at the UK Department of Health

John Scott Cree

Introduction

The Department of Health (DH) Library and Information Services (LIS) exists to meet the operational and strategic information needs (including training, education and material on work-related matters) of DH staff. There are approximately 5000 members of staff in multiple sites across the country, including the National Health Service Executive. Services are provided by 43 staff in four libraries in London and Leeds which are stocked with approximately 200,000 books and pamphlets and 2000 current periodicals on key areas of departmental interest – health service management, public health and the personal social services. Frequently-used online services include Justis Parliament, Knight-Ridder Data-Star, DIALOG and MEDLINE services, HMSO and FT Profile. These are supported by CD-ROMs including Parliamentary Database, MEDLINE, Eurolaw, UKOP, HMSO and Global Bookbank.

This chapter will describe, in broad terms, the development of the large, mature network with multiple applications which supports communications within DH, and the process of adding a large integrated library system to that network. Smith[1] provides a full technical description of the DH network as it existed at the time of Unicorn implementation described below·

Automation history

The Department of Health and Social Security (DHSS), as it was then known, was one of the first Government departments to embrace IT.

In 1982 after several years of investigation,[2-5] the DHSS decided to purchase STATUS software on PRIME computer hardware, from British Nuclear Fuels (BNF) Metals Technology Centre, the franchise holder.

When the package became operational on 1 October 1983, a serials management system had been specified as a desirable feature of the operational requirement (OR).[6] However, although originally a secondary priority, the serials database was the first to go online in 1983 and served as a test bed for much of the software, including the development of a loans system.

In July 1984, the main part of the database, DHSS-DATA, which was soon to hold records of approximately 40,000 books, pamphlets, journal articles, Departmental publications and circulars, standards, conference proceedings, research documents and annual reports,[7] was made publicly available via two hosts, SCICON and Data-Star.

A year later, the DHSS Library had automated most of the intended functions with the exception of order chasing,[8] and loans control. It was also hoped that in the near future, menu-driven systems for non-library users would be developed.[9]

In 1989, DHSS split into two departments – Department of Health (DH) and Department of Social Security (DSS). However, DH continued to provide library services to both departments.

By 1992, DH library needed more complex management information than the orders and serials databases were able to provide. Therefore, CAIRS on PRIME was acquired to provide this function, but there were technical problems which took some time to resolve. Moreover, management information was restricted to expenditure on acquisitions. Data of orders entered in CAIRS could not be transferred to STATUS, e.g. to enhance for cataloguing purposes. Despite the anticipation in earlier published articles, loans had not yet been automated and, although access to STATUS was possible in theory for all Departmental staff over the Office Information System (OIS), the proposed menu-driven systems for non-library users had not been developed and, in practice, the front end was insufficiently user-friendly to encourage use by more than a few non-library staff.

Also by 1992 there were major changes elsewhere in DH, particularly location moves and the beginning of market testing of non-core functions against private sector competition.[10] A large part of the DH's business, involving 1000 civil servants concerned mainly with the then NHS Management Executive (NHSME), had transferred to Leeds. This had justified the business case for the OIS which links all Departmental staff to one computer network. Figure 5.1 gives a simplified view of OIS at November 1996, after the addition of regional offices. OIS is linked by ethernet local-area networks within buildings and, between buildings, via a router WAN which consists of high-speed leased circuits linking resilient dual operational routers in five main buildings. Other sites are connected by site routers and leased bearers. OIS runs on a server platform of more than 100 Netware 3.11 servers. Links to host computers use TCP/IP.

As well as the urgent need to ensure that good communications were set up between the London and Leeds communities, the facility was required to transfer documents as easily as possible between geographically disparate sections within the same division. Supplemented by video conferencing facilities, OIS was installed in the DH estate over 24 months, which was believed to be a very short timescale considering the numbers of staff involved and the fact that many of them were in the process of moving from one part of the country to another.

Part of the moves included the establishment of a library service for NHSME and DSS staff in Quarry House, Leeds, and of a service for NHS Estates in Trevelyan Square, Leeds. Both were able to access STATUS over OIS.

One consequence of the short installation timescale imposed by the Leeds move, was that considerations of the use of OIS as a means of disseminating cor-

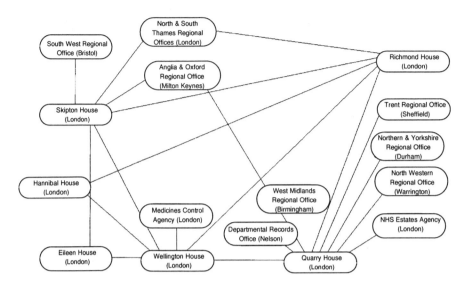

Fig. 5.1 *OIS – a simplified view*

porate information, were left until later, while the more immediate requirements of training and supporting users in word-processing and mail facilities
took priority, to enable users to send and receive ASCII, WordPerfect and
binary files (or any combination of these) across the system. In 1993, DH's
Information Services Directorate (ISD) issued a Document and Information
Management Strategy (DIMS) paper. DIMS recommended the development of
appropriate policies, procedures and systems for document management and
the development of corporate sources of information using the existing OIS
infrastructure. As well as Windows-based, location-independent access to standard word-processing (WordPerfect 5.1 initially, 5.2 from 1995) and mail
(Route400) and a bespoke staff location database, individual users or groups of
users have network access to a variety of products, including spreadsheets, desktop publishing and statistical/financial modelling packages. Initially standard
character-based workstations (386 or 486 PC) provided a standard menu interface for access to these applications, including terminal emulation, on a number
of host computers including the PRIME minicomputer, Amdahl mainframe,
ICL mainframe and various UNIX systems. The growing need for task switching or use of Windows applications resulted, after a successful pilot, in roll-out
across DH of OIS II implementing Windows 3.1 in 1995. By this date, the
Unicorn implementation described later was proceeding and, concurrently,
work was in progress elsewhere in ISD under DIMS to put up a Press Index
Service, a Hansard Summary Service and Electronic Directory of Business,
with a view to speeding up the amount of routine information distributed across
the Department and to offer a more efficient use of disk capacity than large-

scale mail distributions. At the same time, savings, in the form of staff no longer required for manual distribution, savings in the print budget and in numbers of subscriptions to Hansard were identified. Work was also on-going to network CD-ROMs successfully. This on one of the largest computer networks in Whitehall meant that, by the end of 1995, most Departmental business and electronic communication was carried out on OIS.

Selection of a new library system

Following a successful in-house bid in the market test exercise of 1993 and the subsequent service level agreement between the library and the Department, a review of library housekeeping and information retrieval systems by PA Consulting in April 1994 recommended replacement of existing PRIME-based, non-integrated library systems and listed appropriate suppliers.

Library and information services (LIS) form part of ISD. A project (PEx) board consisting of representatives from other branches of ISD was set up. Figure 5.2 shows in outline how ISD was organized at December 1994. A consultant project manager was appointed to oversee the preparation of a user requirements specification for acquisitions, cataloguing, end-user searching, loans, interlibrary loans, serials acquisition and circulation, current awareness and seamless searching of external databases.

ISD 1	ISD 2	ISD 3	ISD 4	ISD 5	ISD 6	ISD 7
Finance	Mainframe services and applications	Helpdesk	Document & Information Management Strategy (DIMS)	IT strategy and standards	Financial and administrative system	OIS implementation for NHS Executive Regional Offices
Administration		OIS managment		User support		
Procurement	Project management liaison and support	Change management	Libraries & Information Services (LIS)	Services and commissioning		
Contract management		E-mail				
Service level management	Requirements analysis and small systems development	Central LAN management and UNIX support	Staff location database	Finance & procurement management		
Personnel policy for IT staff	Business support	Technical projects	Distribution of business	OIS II Programme management		
IT security		Video conferencing	Distribution lists			
Data Protection Act		Telecommunications	Departmental records			
Project office and quality management			Corporate data administration			

Fig. 5.2 *The organization of ISO in December 1994*

Project-based IT procurement for DH was performed using the Central Computer and Telecommunications Agency (CCTA)'s PRINCE methodology[11] where appropriate. This included use of the previously mentioned project board and project manager and the drawing up of a project implementation plan with a time/action chart for the software supplier, the library and the hardware supplier divided across weeks and showing milestone activities for each (e.g. data conversion and training), at verifiable points in the project. Procurement itself was by means of a call-off contract with Siemens-Nixdorf (SNI), who sent the user requirement to suppliers. Site visits and demonstrations were arranged while proposals were worked up by suppliers. SNI produced an options analysis study to evaluate suppliers' written proposals and, in October 1994, Sirsi's Unicorn product emerged as the preferred option. Unicorn met the largest number of user requirements as well as the DH strategic requirement for a Windows-based application, although it was available in character version also. In late November 1994, I was recruited as senior librarian project manager to manage the software supplier part of the implementation and to oversee data conversion.

System specification

All staff were able to contribute to the user requirement specification, through

- interviews
- observation of their work by those from ISD responsible for drawing up the user requirement document
- opportunities to respond to draft versions of the document
- cross-library quality control meetings to determine the necessary weighting of each requirement
- smaller focus group meetings of assistant librarians and librarians, both under the chairmanship of the project manager.

The result was an extremely detailed document which listed 174 mandatory and desirable requirements but which, including subdivisions, amounted to more than 1000 requirements. Many of these were based on long experience of STATUS and a desire to see its features replicated in the new system. Two examples of subdivided requirements will illustrate this.

Requirement 0010 to 'input provisional orders' showed current provision as

> Input to work file – not shown on catalogue until after overnight batch update. Orders can be created on the CAIRS Book Catalogue File (LIBO) with loan and cataloguing information, but not all details are carried through reliably to other processes.

Required provision was expressed as

- online update of integrated database *mandatory*
- from any branch library (stock) or by Procurement Liaison Unit (. . . retention

copies for library users)

- create order skeleton from scratch or using in-house or imported catalogue information (publisher, BNB, BLCMP etc) *mandatory*
- multiples of an item up to 99999, financial extensions to match
- once a provisional order has been created, details of the item and its order status should be visible to anyone browsing or searching the catalogue (show order date, number of copies ordered, date(s) required and destined locations – information on intended recipients of retention copies should be available as an option) *mandatory*
- spell-check input against dictionary that can recognize specialist titles and authors (dictionary might be fed from thesaurus) *desirable*
- validate ISBN format *mandatory*
- record any bibliographic information available – price, destination(s) of copies purchased, budget/cost code, urgent/non-urgent requirement (priority code), employee code (person raising/entering the order), borrower ID for person reserving or requesting for retention, loan reservation details, notes on cataloguing *mandatory*
- orders may be for items to be received at multiple locations, with full allocation of costs by site and budget; some costs may need to be apportioned between cost centres *mandatory*.

In terms of managing user expectations, my previous experience suggested that Sirsi's Functional Requirement Response was correct in answering a simple 'yes' that Unicorn would do the following:

- Update the database online. However, it would not immediately update indexes to permit immediate searching and retrieval of an item. Retrieval was possible only if the control number created by the system was known and used. Indexes were updated by halting and running the system and creating update reports. In practice, indexes could not be updated during the working day, but by running overnight reports on the system.
- Operate a spell check. However, this would be only by running an overnight report on the system.
- Validate ISBN format. However, this would be only by running an overnight report on the system.

A second example is that of requirement 0270 'management reports'. Required provision was expressed as

Journals
1 listing of journals supplied to division/cost centre code/library service point
2 cost of journal subscriptions by division/cost centre code/library service point
2a costs to include both actual expenditure and/or committed expenditure for new subscriptions
3 list of journals by subject covered

4   details of new subscriptions placed during any given period

Standing orders

1   list of standing orders by the same categories as above
2   cost of standing orders, again both actual expenditure and committed
     expenditure

Books

1   listing of orders by requester
2   costs (as above)
3   details of outstanding orders
4   details of supply times by supplier.

All these rated as one *mandatory* and there was, in addition, in the one requirement 0270

Overall spending

1   expenditure with each supplier per month, quarter, year *desirable.*

In terms of a user requirement specification, there are clearly several mandatory
and desirable features which, in turn, may be subdivided into other functions
subsumed within one requirement.

I wished to avoid the situation where all of these multifaceted requirements
became acceptance tests to be added as schedules to any contract. I therefore
sought and obtained the agreement of the PEx board, that, for contract purposes, the level of acceptance testing to be specified would be adequate to ensure
that the software performed as expected, but that detailed testing to confirm the
function and operation of every module and facility would be carried out over
an extended period of time after roll-out to all users. The user requirement specification staff were then revisited in all sections involved with each module and
they were asked to identify requirements for acceptance testing in these terms.
This resulted in a more manageable list of about 50 requirements.

The business case, as it was approved, projected a concurrent user population
of 120, drawn across OIS from all DH library sites plus those of its agencies –
Medicines Control Agency, NHS Estates Agency and Medical Devices Agency
– together with a specialized Divisional information unit and, in the following
financial year, roll-out of the OPAC to all DH staff across OIS. SNI specified a
dedicated Sunsparc host for Unicorn, as being most hospitable to growth.
Additionally, a redundant array of inexpensive disks (RAID) system was
selected as offering the best technology for getting the system up and running
in the event of hard disk failure or corruption. A Data General Clariion RAID
system supporting RAID 5, which guarantees integrity of data should any disk
fail, was chosen. This provides just under 3GB of extremely robust data storage.
The Clariion can be configured to support hot spares, which means that a failed
disk can be replaced in real time without having to switch off the unit. This is
to enable LIS to meet the service level agreements (SLAs) which it has operated

with DH since winning the market test exercise in 1993 and which, because of the urgent nature of requests for information – often from Ministerial level – include 98% system availability.

System test procedures, which are necessary before adding any new application to OIS, are described below. For this purpose, DH procured loan models of Sunsparc and RAID. It was envisaged that a firm order would keep these in place if testing were successful. SNI agreed partitioning with Sirsi, then passed this to the department's UNIX team for direct contact with Sirsi on the system build.

The desktop PC with the highest specification in DH then was 486, although the majority were 386. Sirsi warned that the GUI version of their Unicorn product would have trouble running on a 386, so a short-term move to the character version seemed to have merit. However, the long-term commitment had to be to the GUI version. Fortuitously, this project coincided with a DH network upgrade project (OIS II) and a DH decision to standardize on Pentium PCs.

Data conversion

It was decided before the system was selected that the bibliographic database, DHSS-DATA, would be converted from STATUS. In addition, user records would be converted from CAIRS, but serial and order records would not be converted, as data quality was not always consistent.

To enable staff to be trained on data they recognized, a conversion or, in this case, migration of DHSS-DATA was made by Sirsi before training commenced. Sirsi were to make a second pass at migration after training and before 'live' date, to include all input transactions made to STATUS since the first pass and to redefine any conversion rules which had resulted in identifiable problems.

I had two previous experiences of data migration at the Department of the Environment (DoE). First, in 1992 the DoE's BLAISE/LOCAS file had been inverted for searching on BLAISE-LINE. Some difficulties were encountered with local UKMARC tag 950 which contained information on the number of copies of an item held at each of 18 locations, together with accession numbers, some shelfmark information and natural language strings on copies missing or shelved at reference, etc. The company which performed the inversion, wrote in November 1992 that the 'few odd words [in these strings] shouldn't get in anyone's way', although an early attempt to find a solution to the problem would have resulted in the disappearance of punctuation from classmarks. This was resolved by February 1993.

Second, in October 1993, DoE had decided to procure Sirsi's Unicorn system. In due course, data migration from BLAISE-LINE to Unicorn had worked well, apart from in one significant area – the location/holdings information held formerly in the 950 tag. In Unicorn this information is held outside the bibliographic record and conversion to Unicorn could not cope with the natural language strings in the field. As a result, all holdings were made to default to one copy at HQ. This was perceived initially by staff as being one irritant among several with the new system which would need to be lived with. Holdings were the same across libraries on many items, particularly of official publications. However, the implications of not knowing the holdings of individual libraries became more apparent as use of the system grew, although by this time sufficient new data had been added to make reconversion unhelpful. The assumption was that this would be less of an issue as these holdings became more historic and of less immediate relevance.

Having transferred to DH, I discussed with the Senior Management team the merits or otherwise of 'big bang' or 'direct' data conversion/migration.

Four methods of changeover had been identified by Brewin[12] in his internal DHSS report on pre-automation library practice and recommendations for post-automation practice. First, the 'direct' method, i.e. one day the old system, next day the new system. This had the advantages of no extra staff costs and rapid changeover. Disadvantages were seen as the high risk, the need for total system confidence and user expertise, and the conversion of the dynamic data of records subject to change. Second, Brewin identified 'parallel running', i.e. both systems running for a given period of time. Advantages were seen as the very low risk and the feasibility of direct comparison. Disadvantages were the high cost in resources, the availability or otherwise of skilled staff, the problem of deciding when to make the changeover and the fact that users continued to have fall-back confidence in the old system. The third method identified by Brewin was that of 'phased changeover' or pilot running, i.e. a gradual change-over of specific functions until total system changeover. The advantage of this is that it is possible to revert to the original system. Disadvantages are the duplication of staff effort, the restricted possibilities of data comparison, the difficulty of controlling the momentum of changeover and finally, the high risk. The fourth method is what Brewin calls 'retrospective parallel running', i.e. the conversion of old material to the new system to test it. Advantages of this are low commitment and low risk at changeover. Disadvantages are that the new system is not behaving in real time, comparison is difficult, there are high staff costs and there is the temptation never to change.

Brewin asserted that the solution to the conversion problem might involve any or all of the alternatives he had identified.

I had experience of two successful direct conversions and argued successfully in favour of this, although there was, subsequently, some parallel running to mop up existing orders in acquisitions and to allow for the separate migration of serials data mentioned later. A list of tags used in STATUS was requested and preliminary data mappings were made. By reference again to Brewin's report, it was apparent that decisions on punctuation had been made to accord with AACR2 and, on choice of tags, to tie local practice as closely as possible to UKMARC, with two notable exceptions.

First, the holdings tag, which described the number of copies of an item held in each library site, contained natural language in the form 'Filed in series', 'Not in stock', 'Reference', 'Missing', etc. As a result of DoE experience, all DH,

DSS and Agency staff were asked through the Data Quality Circle to recall, search and identify any such terms. Holdings data were copied to a notes tag in STATUS to allow staff continuity in using STATUS, then global edits were made to remove natural language from the data still held at the holdings tag. The reason for this is that, without clean holdings/location data at the conversion stage, it is not possible to create separate libraries for each site in Unicorn nor add the copies each library holds of an item.

The second exception concerned authors, who were held in separate fields depending on whether the item was a monograph or a journal article. These were simple enough to combine and map to appropriate UKMARC tags. The problem arose where there were multiple authors. The AACR2 concept of up to three authors had been followed in part by putting field delimiters around them. However, where there were more than three authors, practice had been to put 'et al' after the first, followed by field delimiter then the names of all additional authors. Personal authors had been input in one continuous string and corporate authors had been entered on separate lines (within the same field) divided by line forcing symbols, also surrounded by markers to determine the name to be shown prominently at the head of records in printed bibliographies or bulletins. Global edits were made in STATUS to try to ensure consistency of punctuation and spacing within tags. These global edits, like those of holdings data, had to be done over a period of time as the system could cope only with a total of 500 such edits each night.

Discussions were then held with Sirsi to agree understanding of rules which would cover the conversion of natural language punctuation to UKMARC subfield indicators. Sirsi were also helpful in devising rules, for example, to create UKMARC second indicators for stop words. However, Unicorn's use of USMARC features means that subfield markers do not convert to punctuation in the OPAC. There is a blank where punctuation or subfield marker ought to be, which results in some confusing word strings particularly in the title field. USMARC requires that punctuation be wastefully double-keyed with subfield markers, to permit its display in the OPAC. However, DH took the decision to follow UKMARC practice and key only subfield markers, in the expectation that a growing body of UK Unicorn users would demand from Sirsi their automatic conversion to punctuation, as well as to facilitate future record import/export. This was before the issue became a prominent debating point in the British Library's MARC harmonization proposals, whose outcome is awaited (November 1996).

When all was ready, records were transferred by file transfer protocol (FTP) from STATUS on PRIME to the Sunsparc host (named 'Hercules' by ISD).

Departmental implementation procedures

To add any application to the DH network, a request for change control must be approved. This includes testing on a Reference Network (REFNET). However, at the time REFNET was to be run, DHSS-DATA had not been converted and staff had not received training in Unicorn. Sirsi therefore loaded their test database of 50,000 records, then gave a group of staff an overview of modules and afterwards assisted them in performing basic tasks on a restricted part of the network which would permit REFNET monitoring. In the absence of acquisitions or loans data, significant reports from these modules were unable to be run in the background, and staff were effectively limited to creating items, users, loans, etc. and information retrieval from an unfamiliar database, with varying complexity of searches. REFNET testing indicated minimal traffic across the network and was successful from the point of view of network safeguards. However, it failed to identify two significant problems.

First, it was not readily apparent that there were problems exiting cleanly from the GUI version of the Unicorn Workstation. Processes were left running on the UNIX host which eventually caused the system to fall over after a series of on-screen error messages during training sessions in early February and again in March 1995. Although pentiums were now largely in place, the decision was then taken to proceed with the character version of Unicorn. These problems with the GUI Workstation instability were resolved and new software was delivered in spring 1995. At the time of writing (November 1996), the character version is still in place. There have been some discussions between the UNIX team and Sirsi on the means the GUI uses to access the host. Sirsi favours Windows sockets with logins managed by the application, whereas the UNIX team required individual telnet sessions, to permit use of existing user accounting software.

A resolution is also required to a consequential difficulty arising from the second problem not identified at REFNET testing – that the DH host-based standard TCP/IP interface, LAN Workplace for DOS version 4, could not support the Workstation software for Unicorn. LAN Workplace for DOS version 4.2 was necessary, but because it was not a Departmental standard and had not itself been subjected to change control procedures, it had to be installed on each of the 70 PCs in the initial roll-out. The consequential problem is that each PC needs to be visited for each OIS update, to resolve any clashes in applications which may, for example, prevent access to the library database (now renamed Library and Information Online Network or LION) or printer access. Work is in progress to mount LAN Workplace for DOS 4.2 on network servers. At the same time, the mounting of Sirsi's GUI and TY software on each PC requires each user to download update and upgrade files to their local (c:) drive through an update utility in Unicorn. Efforts are being made to have these network server-mounted too, as the support overhead of visiting each PC for fault diagnosis and resolution or installation of new users is clearly not viable. Mention should also be made at this stage of a pilot project to roll out desktop Internet access to 50 workstations which has identified a clash between the .DLL used for this and the .DLL used for Unicorn GUI.

Telecommunications

LIS also has service level agreements with a number of DH Executive Agencies and, until 1 April 1996, with the DSS. Together with provision of library services such as cataloguing and acquisitions, agreements include access to LION for details of library holdings and journal articles. Most of these non-LIS users are not on the OIS network, but have access to LION via the PRIME over Xyplex links (see Figure 5.3). Tests indicated that it was not possible to access the GUI version of Unicorn over Xyplex, but there was no problem with accessing the character-based version, which it had already been decided to implement for the reasons outlined above.

Printers

All OIS users have access to a network printer (see Figure 5.3), generally located in or near their business area. Since most of these are not the latest model, they are configurable either as network or as local printers, but not as both. Netjet cards, which permit both IP and IPX access, were ordered for the 12 existing library printers used by staff across the various sites. Some applications, e.g. printing labels for journal routing, need to be executed locally, hence the need for both access routes.

Human issues

Through visits to each site and by use of e-mail, I made early contact with all staff to explain how differently Unicorn would perform and to persuade staff of the benefits, e.g. in the vastly improved speed of searching. DHSS-DATA had been designed for subject searching, including the use of pre-explosions to

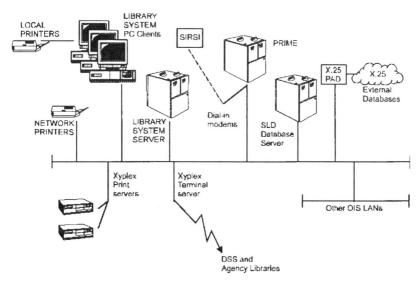

Fig. 5.3 *Library system network on 9 May 1995*

denote the broad subject slant of an item and to increase the relevancy of online searches.[13] It had also been possible to search on specific fields, including free text searching of abstracts and searching by publication type, e.g. circulars, DH/DSS series or government series. However, searching was very slow where large numbers of relevant documents were identified. It subsequently transpired that input into relevant 'chapters', e.g. of departmental publications for official use only, had been inconsistent, with a consequent incomplete searching facility. Searching was much quicker in Unicorn and a search on 'health', for example, produced 59,000 references in less than two seconds. It was then possible to refine a large search result by item type 'circular', or 'press release' as well as by year of publication, library, etc. as necessary. This was of particular importance for those members of staff who had not had the benefit of site visits and acquired, for handouts, multiple copies of Sirsi literature which featured screen dumps.

To monitor staff response and progress in the subsequent Sirsi training programme I sat in with staff on the training sessions and, prior to going live, I prepared a frequent but irregular newsletter entitled *LIONnews* for sending across OIS and in hard copy to Agencies and DSS. This kept staff informed of developments and sought to give hints and to answer queries by means of a 'problem page'.

In the post-market test environment, LIS had regular meetings of a computer user group to discuss issues relating to STATUS and CAIRS, and of a data quality circle to make decisions where there were variations in the interpretation of input instructions. As the project neared implementation in March 1995, some staff faced with the inevitability of change experienced the well-documented low point in morale which, unfortunately, coincided with fragmentation of the training programme because of system instability described elsewhere in this chapter. I was concerned that the interim solution of converting only 50,000 mainly non-DH test records (described later), meant that records were largely unfamiliar to users and the conversion appeared less elegant than the first pass of 20 January. Problems continued to be identified, but the absence of the total database meant that fewer problems could be seen. I therefore presented a briefing paper 'Why we are where we are' to the computer user group and took part in an open discussion forum.

Concern had also been expressed that the lack of embedded punctuation in the OPAC should have been discovered at site visits and, similarly, about the need to involve all acquisitions staff to avoid the possibility of repetition of problems with a previous acquisitions module. I explained that evaluation criteria for selection of the system did not require that every item in the user specification be met. Similarly, all library systems were stronger in some modules (usually the one around which each was built) than in others and Unicorn would not be rejected solely because it was found to be less satisfactory in one module than in another. However, the requirements for each module had been drawn up by sections responsible for their implementation, and they must now decide which were the most important for functionality acceptance tests after completion of the training programme.

The Senior Management Team consisting of Senior Librarians in Customer Services London and Leeds, Senior Librarian Quality Resource Management and myself, decided to build on computer user groups and data quality circles by appointing function groups to oversee working practices on each LION module and to draw up written procedures. Function Groups consist of staff, led by Librarians, working in relevant sections of LIS and the other libraries with membership drawn from all sites. There continue to exist (November 1996) groups on acquisitions, cataloguing, data input, information retrieval, serials and SDI/bulletin and, as experts on their module, they act as first point of reference for queries from staff relating to that module, as well as reporting to computer user group which has now been renamed LION User Committee. An additional function group is likely to take responsibility for circulation and interlibrary loans.

Training

To gain maximum benefit from Unicorn as an integrated library system, most modules with an input element require staff to become de facto cataloguers. Short in-house sessions for inputters were held on UKMARC coding of author, title and publication details, with fuller sessions for cataloguers. At the same time, Sirsi devised a training session on basic data input (simplified cataloguing) for staff involved with acquisitions, loans of uncatalogued items, etc.

After consultation with staff, a one-month training programme with Sirsi was arranged. Sirsi were to deliver to staff, in relevant work units, training in OPAC, cataloguing, data input as mentioned earlier, acquisitions, loans and systems administration. Training was scheduled to commence two months before going live. On the Friday before training was due to commence, the PCs earmarked for training purposes arrived at lunchtime just as the fork-lift truck broke down, the driver went to lunch and the snow began falling. Resilient library staff commandeered a flat-bed trolley and unloaded 12 pallets of IT equipment and had them securely housed within the library in double quick time. A training room was then rapidly networked by ISD colleagues and the five training PCs configured, including slowing the pentium processor speed for Unicorn GUI, ready for the start on Monday.

Subsequently the GUI problems outlined earlier, manifested themselves and several training sessions were severely fragmented. Training continued with the character version and at this point, the training programme with Sirsi was revisited. It was agreed that it would be more beneficial for staff for the programme to continue, where appropriate, with workshop-based question and answer sessions, rather than with the standard scripted approach and this proved to be the case.

Installation of the new system

REFNET testing by ISD technical support, system configuration by ISD's UNIX team with Sirsi, conversion by Sirsi of approximately 120,000 records held previously in DHSS-DATA on STATUS and the beginning of the training programme had all been carried out on a rental Sunsparc machine. It was not possible, as had been envisaged, to retain the rental machine and RAID box. However, the arrival and configuration of the permanent replacement host was complicated by the failure of the SOLARIS back-up of the rental host. Although the UNIX team worked over a weekend to install the system and reload Unicorn data, there were problems reading back-up tapes. It transpired that there was a bug in SOLARIS 2.3, which corrupted back-up data and for which DH had not received a fix. There was also an error in ISD's back-up script which meant that no data were being backed up in any event. As a result, scheduled back-ups were not performing correctly and verification of nothing or 'nil data' had been occurring, so the fault was not discovered beforehand. The silver lining here was the timely discovery of this fault which enabled it to be rectified on other Sunsparc machines to which DH was upgrading. Sirsi worked quickly to reconfigure the replacement host and to install the only readable records, which were 50,000 Sirsi test records, to allow for reduced server capacity until the replacement RAID box arrived. (In the event, training was to be completed using these 50,000 records.) After an unsatisfactory OPAC training session which used only Harvard screens, the training programme was able to resume, albeit with the as yet unidentified GUI problems and the consequent fragmentation of a number of training sessions.

Sirsi subsequently ran system reliability tests using projections of growth and peak transactions over a five-year period. However, this exercise was run only on the host and not across the network. DH recognized the difficulty of incorporating response times into acceptance tests on a network which utilized differing communications solutions and whose growth could not be predicted. Subsequently, there were some problems with system stability as kernel parameters were experimented with by Sirsi in consultation with the UNIX team. I kept records of all downtime using black spots on a year planner, as previous experience of a similar project, with differing hardware and software suppliers, had shown the effectiveness of using this as a demonstration tool in discussions.

DH went live with acquisitions, cataloguing and OPAC Unicorn modules on 9 May 1995.

It became apparent that some problems of data conversion resulted from inconsistencies in choice of tag, punctuation or spacing in original STATUS input. However, the main problem occurred where multiple corporate authors converted in a single string or sub-bodies did not have full stop + space converted to ¦c. (¦ is the Unicorn equivalent of the MARC $ subfield marker.) In some cases ¦c was inserted, but the full stop + space remained in front of it instead of being substituted, while in other cases the full stop + space stayed just as it was with no ¦c appearing. Moreover, authors long enough to run onto a second line in STATUS had a colon inserted at the point where the line run-over occurred. There had been a second pass by Sirsi at the conversion, after completion of the training programme, to incorporate STATUS data input subsequent to the first data migration. However, the extent of the multiple corporate author problem in tag 710 had not been measured fully by that stage. Work has continued in DH to amend problematic entries by hand. There was also a need to remap appropriate STATUS data in the 008 tag. This had been done originally using UKMARC subfields, whereas Unicorn fixed field 008 data were in nonconfigurable USMARC subfields, and this had resulted in incorrect location of publication date(s) and government publication data.

Orders were input to LION from live date and existing orders were allowed to progress through CAIRS until completion. Subsequently, Sirsi converted data relating to approximately 2000 serial titles plus subscriptions, taken electronically from the files of Ebsco, the library supply contractors. This produced substantial savings in the time staff would have needed to spend inputting the records. Serials check-in and circulation were maintained on CAIRS until work was completed on routeing lists on LION in December 1995. DH changed nomenclature from 'circulation' to 'routeing' and from 'loans' to 'circulation' to conform with standard practice.

Circulation and routeing both require good user data. Taken initially from CAIRS data, these were found to be unsatisfactory. Users and their old locations had never been deleted from the system, in order to provide an historical record which would enable users and their replacements to be identified for outstanding orders, serials routeing, etc. As a result, there were in excess of 13,000 records for about 5000 staff. It was therefore decided to replace the CAIRS user records with records from the staff location database, which is managed by LIS and mentioned earlier. After live date, the circulation module became available, as well as a working model of bulletin production.

Sirsi also carried out work to convert the DH thesaurus (held previously in STATUS with Stride software) to the Unicorn authority file and to build into the authority file the names of corporate authors and subject keywords. The data conversion problem mentioned earlier, where multiple corporate authors have converted in a single string, has produced some odd-looking authorities which have been used to assist in the manual cleaning of tag 710 data. However, the nonconversion of subbodies has resulted in many records finishing at the full stop before the subbody and hence a number of duplicate authority records, for example

University of Durham. Department of Engineering

becomes in authority

University of Durham.

and duplicates other departments of the University which similarly have not converted. It also stamps 'unauthorized' records which legitimately have

University of Durham as author, but which lack this full stop.

There was an initial difficulty with the thesaurus in that the classmark was mixed in with the related terms (which is still the case in display), but it was resolved so that the distinction was clearly made, at least when editing. The major problem with the thesaurus was that non-preferred synonyms were made into separate records instead of having a shadowy existence only by virtue of being in the 400 'use for' field of the preferred term. The independently existing non-preferred corporate author records had the effect of wrongly authorizing the unwanted forms in the 689 subject keyword field (e.g. United States instead of United States of America). Problems arose when we asked for them to be deleted, as tag 410 is 'see/use' in subject authority records, whereas in the corporate authority 410 is the tag for 'see from/use for'. Every corporate authority record with a 'see from' entry was wiped out when the thesaurus was corrected. On three occasions DH conducted cleaning exercises in authority for 'Department of Health', 'Department', 'Ministry', 'Royal College of . . . ', universities by name and all their subbodies, but records reverted to incorrect form when the file was rebuilt.

A related problem arising from the authorizing of non-preferred forms is that because the corresponding bibliographical records were once authorized, they do not display as UNAUTHORIZED (until they are edited), even though the false justification for their authorization has been removed.

It appears that authority records are held in the system in C-ISAM files which do not display. The Unicorn authority file sits in BRS Search and selects one C-ISAM record on which to build the authority. Authority records have been amended manually, but a duplicate may reappear when the authority file is rebuilt. We are working with Sirsi to remove these duplicates to solve the problem. Sirsi have set up a report to enable DH to search for duplicates. Sirsi previously produced three long lists of duplicate authority records which DH edited, but which reverted to earlier forms on rebuilding the authority file. However, since being given the facility to produce the reports in-house, we have not seen evidence for the type of reversion to earlier authority record forms which once seemed to be happening.

One benefit of the Unicorn implementation is that all input is now standardized on UKMARC format. However, this meant additional work to achieve satisfactory weekly data export to Knight-Ridder, now responsible for Data-Star access to DHSS-DATA (subsequently renamed DH data after the establishment of a separate DSS library service on 1 April 1996).

Regional offices (ROs)

A result of NHS reforms was the establishment, on 1 April 1996, of Regional Offices (ROs) of the NHS Executive to replace Regional Health Authorities. In the period since going live with Unicorn, the role of libraries in these ROs has become more clearly defined and the Unicorn OPAC has been rolled out to all. Each RO library has been visited to examine existing library data on their various CAIRS, Soutron, Inmagic and Access systems, for possible conversion to LION. Reports have been prepared of work which needs to be done to clean their data prior to conversion. Appropriate hardware upgrades were procured to accommodate an additional seven RO libraries in Unicorn. Each 'library' sits in BRS Search and the addition of RO libraries was not envisaged at the time the system was sized in 1994. With the upgrades in place and data cleaned and converted, the cataloguing module will be rolled out to RO libraries. At the time of writing, North Thames RO data has been added to LION. The North Thames catalogue of approximately 3000 records was run against LION to identify duplicates. The location THA was added in LION to identify each of these 'duplicates' and the remaining original records were added separately to LION. A similar exercise is being conducted with the specialized divisional information unit mentioned earlier, which previously maintained its own database on STATUS.

Future developments

Roll-out of modules requiring bespoke work, has been protracted. Although there were difficulties resourcing this within the DH systems administration team while the system was being bedded down with users, this seems also to be the result of a lack of demand in the North American user community for journal routeing, bulletin/SDI and interlibrary loans – hence lack of development of these areas. There seems to be more concern with high profile areas like GUI and WebCat access. Additionally, the systems administration team is reluctant to embark on bespoke work which, Sirsi have warned the Unicorn User Group, may not be sustainable in future upgrades to the system. The appropriate function groups are being asked to re-examine their part in the user requirement specification and to define more closely those requirements in the light of this and of experience with the system.

Once bedding-down procedures and the RO dimension become history, development work can proceed on modules such as interlibrary loans, SDI (the profiled information service) and the Unicorn Webcat module (which has replaced the RIM module for seamless searching of external databases). It was intended to roll out the OPAC to the 5000 OIS users in 1996–7, but other departmental IT priorities and the clash on the OIS network of the GUI version with the application for desktop Internet access, are likely to delay this.

Conclusions

Lessons for others are dependent on the variables of timescale and resources in different libraries. DH library has been fortunate over the years in being part of a department which, in the 1970s sought applications to add to its mainframe computer, which provided hardware upgrades and recognized the necessity for management information software in the 1980s, and which advocated implementation of an integrated system in the 1990s. The library further benefited from being part of ISD, which was developing communications and networks links during this period.

As a general principle, migration to a new system will be smoother if user expectation is managed from the outset to ensure a realistically-sized user requirements specification of, at most 150–200 requirements, including subdivisions. Quality assurance of the specification should ensure that requirements are described broadly and that functionality is not listed, so that there will be minimal need for bespoke system tailoring, especially where this is to be used solely to mirror existing practice. To avoid disappointment of users and protracted (hence, costly) implementation and to encourage new ways of thinking, the opportunity should be taken to see where existing practice can be tailored instead to the proposed system. This will be of particular significance in any future system upgrades by the supplier, which may be unable to accommodate or sustain previous bespoke work.

In an ideal situation, there will be staff whose only task following data conversion is to check database records with a fine-tooth comb during the training period, with a view to amending, if necessary, the conversion specification before a second pass and live date. In practice, this means staff adept at both old and new systems, who know what they are looking for. It is difficult while the training programme is running, as the training is an end in itself.

It is essential to keep a firm grip on the documentation which will inevitably proliferate during the project period. Where e-mail is used, a copy of everything should be printed. Whatever one chooses not to copy is bound to be referred to as crucial at a later stage. Separate files for communications with software and hardware suppliers should be kept, as well as for internal technical support correspondence and minutes of meetings. It is also a good idea to keep a lever-arch binder (as this will probably be the thickest) of correspondence with library staff, in order to refer back to their concerns (they tend to come up more than once) and how they were answered by systems administration on the last occasion.

Finally I believe that there is a need for the project manager to acquire the discipline of keeping a detailed journal. This will record the timing and outcome of every telephone call, meeting (formal and informal) and e-mail, as well as letters written and documents produced. This will prove to be an invaluable reference tool in any subsequent contentious discussions with suppliers and other main players in the project, who are unlikely to have kept as detailed a record. It may be useful to the project board and line management if it is passed up the line as a weekly update briefing.

The Unicorn proposal met the DH requirement for a GUI product running on a UNIX platform, with standard library modules and additional features like hypertext, external database interface, support for Z39.50 and management information. Although the training programme was fragmented as a result of technical problems which were not identified during evaluation or testing procedures, alternatives were used and are still in place. Work continues to resolve problems with authority control. It is nevertheless true to say that Unicorn was implemented successfully in DH within a relatively short timescale.

References

1   Smith, D. A., 'DIMS brightens DH: document and information strategy at the Department of Health', in Latham, S. (ed.), *Networking and libraries: technical innovation and the transformation of information services*, HMSO, 1994, 7–14.

2   Allum, D., 'DYNIX at the DES', *VINE*, 77, December 1989, 8–15.

3   Kahn, A., 'The Department of Health and Social Security Library in context', *Library Association Medical, Health and Welfare Libraries Group newsletter*, 19, March 1983, 5–26.

4   Cotton, J., 'The DHSS integrated library system', *Health libraries review*, 85 (2), 1985, 170–6.

5   Brewin, P., 'Use of STATUS for housekeeping at the DHSS', *VINE*, 58, March 1985, 3–9.

6   Dua, E. D. and Morgan, D., 'The DHSS serials database', *UK Serials Group newsletter*, 8 (1), June 1986, 34–5.

7   Brewin, P., 'Use of STATUS for housekeeping at the DHSS', *VINE*, 58, March 1985, 3–9.

8   Ibid.

9   Cotton, J., op. cit.

10 Smith, D. A., op. cit.

11 Central Computer and Telecommunications Agency, *PRINCE manual: version 1*, HMSO, 1997, (previously published by Blackwell, 1990).

12 Brewin, P., *Library computerization*, DHSS, 1982.

13 Nurcombe, V. J. (ed.), 'DHSS-DATA', in *British official publications online: a review of sources, services and developments*, Library Association, Information Services Group, Standing Committee on Official Publications, 1990, 25–9.

6 Slagelse Central Library – from BibS to Dansk Data Elektronik

Vibeke Hvidtfeldt and Aksel G. Mikkelsen

Introduction

The municipality of Slagelse lies on the Danish island of Zealand and covers an area of 9000 hectares. The town of Slagelse is situated approximately 90 km from Copenhagen and has a population of 30,000 with a further 5000 in the surrounding areas. The most important industry in the rural districts is farming and many farm-related industries are to be found in Slagelse. The town is also noted for being a good market town and is visited by people from far and wide. Finally, the town is also characterized by its many educational institutions: a secondary school, a technical school, a business school, a school for nurses, a teaching college (for those intent on careers in kindergartens, youth clubs, social institutions, etc.).

Slagelse is part of the county of West Zealand which has a population of 290,000, divided amongst 23 municipalities. Each municipality has its own local council, which, for many areas, has the authority to decide what kind of service the residents of the municipality will be offered. The local council decides the standard of child care, the organization of sports facilities, the placement of schools and the level of public library facilities. The county of West Zealand is also covered by a county council which has the power of decision in areas such as hospitals and road networks. The Danish Parliament lays down the legal framework and defines competence for the local and county authorities. However, in recent years, the tendency has been for more and more authority to be decentralized and for decisions to be taken at the local level.

The Danish Library Act demands that all municipalities provide for a public library, but does not specify how extensive these services should be. However, the law does demand that the manager of a public library must have a degree in librarianship (Denmark has two schools of librarianship). It is obvious that in a county such as West Zealand where municipalities vary from a population of 35,000 in the largest (Slagelse) to 5200 in the smallest (Stenlille), there are bound to be large variations in library services. These differences are catered for through close cooperation, which is a major characteristic of the Danish public library system. The Danish Library Act 1920 (in fact, Denmark was the first country in the world to legislate on public libraries) was revised as recently as 1993 and is quite specific in stating that all public libraries are open for all who reside in Denmark. The libraries must also ensure that books and other relevant materials are made available, free of charge. In practice, this means that any Danish public library will borrow books from other libraries if a user needs a specific book which is not available at the local library. This interlibrary loans cooperation exists in a network built up around the so-called 'central libraries'.

As just mentioned, all municipalities must provide for a public library. However, the Library Act also states that every county must have a central library. The Minister of Culture decides which libraries are to function as central libraries for the county. Slagelse Public Library has been chosen to act as central library for West Zealand and is, therefore, one of the 14 central libraries in Denmark. As a central library Slagelse has two main parallel objectives. First, the library is the public library for Slagelse municipality. Second, the library acts as the central library for the county, which is obliged to:

- have a collection which acts as a superstructure for the rest of the libraries in the county
- act as a coordinator of the county's library activities
- establish a system for regular transport between the various public libraries in the county
- act as a consultant for the other libraries in the county
- arrange professional meetings and training.

For its role as a central library, Slagelse receives 3 million kroner each year (approximately £300,000) from the state, and Slagelse local council pay the rest for the upkeep of the library (approximately 17 million kroner per annum in 1997).

Slagelse Central Library was founded in 1898 and today has approximately 53 full-time members of staff, 20 of these are librarians, 25 are office staff and 7 are porters, drivers, book replacers and library assistants. The cleaning service is bought in, so these figures do not include cleaning personnel. The library is open for 48 hours each week, Monday to Friday from 10.00 a.m. to 7.00 p.m. and on Saturdays from 10.00 a.m. to 1.00 p.m. As well as the traditional and legally required collections of books, newspapers, journals and reference materials for adults and children which are for use on site or to be borrowed, the library also has a large collection of records and CDs, both classical and modern, for loan. It has also started to build up a collection of video films and CD-ROMs which can be borrowed. Searching the Internet can be carried out from all staff PCs (56 in all) and the library has made available two PCs for the public which offer the opportunity of searching the Internet for free. At present, there are approximately 320,000 items on the new library system and this is expected to rise to 375,000–400,000 items by the time all our manual records are in machine-readable format. (This figure cannot be more precise as it is about 30 years since there was a complete stock count.)

Slagelse Central Library differs from most other libraries of the same size in that it has no branch libraries. However there is close contact with the technical school, the business school, the central hospital, the teaching college and the secondary school, which all have independent library schemes.

Automation history

In the 1980s, Danish public libraries started to show an interest in the potential of computer technology. In the early days, the focus was on cataloguing the library's holdings, which was seen as a simpler and more elegant alternative to card catalogues. A small number of libraries took on a pioneering role – Herning Central Library, in particular, saw how connecting libraries electronically could make interlibrary loans procedures much simpler.

At the same time, the foundations for a union database covering the public libraries were laid down. This database, known as BASIS, took its initial inspiration from the Danish National Bibliography, the libraries' holdings of foreign literature, and various printed catalogues which had, until then, been the most important tools for the libraries when searching for specific literature. BASIS still exists today and although it is still an important source of information and one that is still being built up, it is slowly being replaced by DANBIB, a database which contains information about the holdings of research libraries as well as public libraries. BASIS is available both online and on CD-ROM, while DANBIB can only be accessed online.

Slagelse Central Library installed its first terminals with access to BASIS in 1984 and was therefore early in joining the computer age. However BASIS was really no more than a vastly improved tool for carrying out information searches. What we in reality wanted was to have an online catalogue of local holdings – our imagination did not stretch to automated circulation facilities back in the mid-1980s.

Slagelse Central Library chose its computer system in 1989 when it became clear that there was the political will to grant the extra financial backing. The library chose the BIBlioteks system (BIBS) which was supplied by Scanvest (which has since become part of Olivetti). The system was designed in Sweden and was in use in several relatively small libraries. Slagelse Central Library was the first customer in Denmark and the plan was that the system's translation to Danish conditions and its further development was to take place with the library as an important consultant and partner. In fact, the choice of BIBS was a case of 'love at first sight'. The system was presented at a computer fair and the library management liked it immediately as it was both simple and well arranged. The love affair was not adversely affected when Slagelse Central Library was offered a very competitive price in return for helping with the modification of the system to Danish conditions. This modification process consisted of, among other things, helping with the translation from Swedish to Danish, an operation which was not that easy even though the two languages are fairly similar. One difficulty was that the Danish alphabet contains a number of special characters: æ, ø, and å. Another difficulty arose when library cards began to be issued through the system. Four lines were needed for the address, but the system could only handle three. Although this was a simple change, it took nearly a year before it was modified to meet the library's needs.

The staff were sceptical about BIBS from the start, partly on an emotional level because they had not been included in the decision-making procedure and partly on a professional level because they – paradoxically – saw the system as being too simple. The staff's reservations on the professional level quickly proved to be justified.

The system was implemented in spring 1990 and the latest acquisitions were put on the system from week 16 in 1990. At the same time the card catalogue was closed, so that all materials from before this date were to be found in the card catalogue and everything from week 16 1990 could be found in BIBS. The intention was that the whole book collection should be available in BIBS as soon as possible, but an attempt at this in spring 1991 showed that it would be a monumental task to feed all the entries because, among other things, the computer format BIBS used could not easily be converted. Put simply, the BIBS format was very like a traditional card catalogue record, which was a very simple model compared with a MARC record which had become the standard.

At the same time, the practical experience we were gaining with the system quickly showed that BIBS was not able to live up to the needs of a central library. It became clear that the computer format was a hindrance when cooperating with other public and central libraries, although the daily use of the system showed that the cataloguing module was simple and easy to use for both staff and the public.

Daily use of the system also showed that the further development that Slagelse was supposed to contribute was more akin to basic development. The demands the library made for the system were only slowly being developed. A major problem during this period was that the company was a Danish subsidiary of a Swedish company, who had to approve all development plans.

As a result, plans to create a library system which consisted of cataloguing and issuing modules were abandoned and instead, the library continued just to record all new acquisitions. BIBS became, therefore, a supplement to the traditional card catalogue and more difficulties arose in having two parallel catalogue systems. It was always necessary to have an item's year of publication in mind in order to decide which catalogue to use in a given situation.

In 1992, we started to investigate whether or not it would be sensible to wait for BIBS's further development, with the weaknesses inherent in the system or if it would be appropriate to admit that our first generation system had had a very short life at Slagelse Central Library. The investigation was followed up by various internal and external investigations into specific areas and everything pointed towards the fact that if the library was to live up to its obligations as a central library, with the technological expansion involved, then a change would be the right decision. The final argument was that the library would have to work in the standard format if it was to take its place as the junction in a computer network and BIBS did not live up to this requirement.

Selecting a new system

In autumn 1994, the opportunity arose to change system. Slagelse Council intended to replace its administrative system (accounting, word-processing, administration, etc.) which the library had not been able to access, but of which it had been hoped to become an integrated part. This was the natural opportunity to establish a connection, which seen in the light of the total investment seemed a small amount. For the library, this had a very positive effect in that the library became part of the council tender and was supplied with hardware as part of council purchases.

The most important thing we had learned from purchasing BIBS was that we had failed to specify our needs and requirements properly before investing. It was, therefore, a high priority to analyse our requirements for the system before inviting tenders.

System specifications were drawn up, based partly on experiences from BIBS and partly on advice from other central libraries, who had overtaken us on the information highway and who were able to provide much useful information gleaned from their own experiences. We also received advice from a professional firm to ensure that nothing had been forgotten and to bring to our attention areas where we did not have the knowledge or experience necessary to see problems in advance. Another vital point was the need for a second generation system which was completely developed – we didn't have the energy to be the locomotive a second time round.

In situations such as the one we found ourselves in – conversion from a first to a second generation system – much can be planned, managed, investigated and controlled, but pure luck also plays its part. The luck in this case was that our former deputy librarian had a year earlier been headhunted to Slagelse Council's administration department and given the job of IT manager with the primary responsibility of managing the council's new computer-related purchases. This meant that the library's viewpoints and needs were represented, even if the two key library personnel, the Head Librarian and the Computer Coordinator, were not present at all meetings. In the decision-making process, the library was less involved in reviewing the council administrative system and mostly gave input to a review of the library system. When negotiations with Dansk Data Elektronik (DDE) started, the only representative from the council was the head of the IT department. The result of the tender was that two companies were capable of providing a computer system which lived up to the requirements and DDE was chosen.

The contract with DDE was signed in spring 1995 and broke new ground in Denmark by opting for a facilities management (FM) solution. The usual solution for a library is to purchase its own server. Slagelse chose the solution whereby the server is kept at the company's address – approximately 100 km from Slagelse – and the library pays a fixed annual sum for this FM solution. This has the advantage that it is not the library's problem to upgrade the server as it becomes necessary, and support is provided by the company, something which saves personnel resources.

Installing the new system

During summer 1995, the new network was installed by DDE. BIBS was still being used, so the old network could not be removed. For a long time, there had to be double cabling to some departments. It certainly wasn't pretty, but it worked.

In spring and summer 1995, the data migration was planned. As BIBS had its own format, the bibliographic records could not just be converted to the new system but had to be input from scratch. The project lasted four weeks, during which the library was closed and staff were *absolutely* forbidden to take holiday or become ill! This closed period lasted from 14 August to 9 September 1995 and 185,000 records were entered.

The general public were informed about the period the library would be closed through advertisements in the local papers, notices at the library and notes inserted in books lent before the library closed. However the reading room remained open so the public could come in to read magazines and newspapers and to use the reference section – this was given a high priority because of the large number of students who used this service. It was possible to return library books to the library, but not to borrow books. The library had purchased a copy of the Danish public libraries joint database, BASIS, and this was set up as a help system in the PC network which we used during the campaign. This proved to be very useful. It contained most of the items that had to be catalogued, so they could be downloaded, but of course there were also titles which the library had in other editions than those to be found in BASIS. These titles were put aside to be catalogued later on. At this point, we felt it necessary to have a name for the system and, after much deliberation, library staff decided on MIKKEL, which is the Danish version of Michael (St Michael is the guardian angel of Slagelse and is pictured on the town's coat of arms).

The practical solution for inputting the data was that the whole personnel was divided into groups of two with one PC between them. Each morning, these 'duo' teams were allocated to the various circulation departments and started where the teams from the day before had left off. One of the team members would take books down from the shelves, stick on barcodes and then pass them to the other team member who was at the PC. This member of staff would search the BASIS database and, if a record could be found, the book's barcode was linked to the bibliographic information using a scanner. It was an important part of the strategy that all books which could not immediately be verified were placed to one side for later attention. The view was that as many titles as possible should be put onto the system when the library was closed and so only the uncomplicated ones were dealt with. As mentioned earlier, 185,000 records were recorded on the new database.

Inputting data has continued since then and has not yet been completed. The explanation for this is, of course, that when the library opened again in September 1995 the data inputting had to be done at the same time as the normal routines. It is now a high priority to complete the project and the goal for doing this is summer 1997.

The next large step forward was on 27 February 1996 when we moved over to electronic issuing, giving up the old photocharging system which, for many years, had served us loyally (and sometimes disloyally, e.g. when the film was underexposed or the picture shaken). Some staff had been on training courses in this module, so the transition was painless. But the following months were difficult because again two parallel systems were being operated – this time in the issue module rather than the catalogue module. We were also nervous as the week before we had closed down BIBS and removed the card catalogue from the circulation area. However, we survived.

Human issues

When we look at the transition from first generation to second generation system, it becomes apparent that one of the issues that contributed to the smooth transition was that all the library staff were involved in the project. Energy, good humour, well-planned training and provision of detailed information were all important factors. A 'feel good' committee was given the task of planning surprises along the way. These included cakes for afternoon coffee, ice cream on a summer's day, maintaining a large notice board which showed how far we were in the project and free fresh fruit. The information flow was helped by the introduction of a newsletter, *MIKKEL-Nyt*, which was distributed when the need arose. In the beginning, *MIKKEL-Nyt* was produced frequently, as things were new, but as time went on it appeared less frequently. Publication has now stopped and news about the system is now published in the weekly newsletter for library staff.

During the entire period described in this chapter, from our realization that BIBS did not fully meet the requirements of a central library right up to the present moment when we are still adjusting to the facilities of the DDE system, the conclusion is that it was important for management and staff to feel they were 'in it together'. At times, the problems seemed insurmountable and during such times it was important to be able to support each other in the belief that the new system was one of the best things to happen to the library and that the problems could be solved. In solving these problems, the experience has been a very positive one in that staff have worked together across academic and departmental barriers, and, although a minority of staff have found it difficult to adjust to change, most have been able to increase their self-confidence because they have been able to see solutions.

Training

An important part of the contract was the training of staff in the DDE system. This training took place at DDE's offices in Herlev, approximately 100 km from Slagelse, and was divided into two sections: a general section which everyone participated in and a more specialized section for those who were involved with specialized functions. So, for example, staff on the issue desk received special training in the circulation module, while staff involved in cataloguing were given training in the cataloguing module. The computer skills staff acquired using BIBS were transferable to the new system, which meant that there were few problems in retraining for DDE.

The library management had given a high priority to training sessions, but in retrospect we have to admit that we could have used more and that it could have been tackled differently. For example, more training could have taken place at the library (it is easier and cheaper to move one instructor to Slagelse than to send ten members of staff to DDE's offices, and for some staff it can be an advantage to be on home ground). The timetable for training could have been better planned so that staff received training nearer the time they were expected to begin working with the system. The training DDE delivered was thorough, well prepared and competent, but it was also dense. A three-day training session could be exhausting and things were soon forgotten if the new skills were not put into practice immediately. Although the training was extensive, perhaps we could have used more. An example of this is that the DDE system contains many possibilities for accessing statistical information. We can produce statistics in relation to borrowers (age, sex, address, etc.), gain circulation information relating to types of material (fiction, non-fiction, CDs, children's literature and much more) and produce cross-transaction statistics (i.e. generating comparative reports by library-defined criteria either by single element or combination) but these were all features we had to teach ourselves.

The need for training is never ending. MIKKEL will keep developing, new versions of the library system will be introduced, we will discover new ways of doing things and new job functions will appear. All this demands that we are prepared to learn new things continuously and the library's Computer Coordinator has taken on the responsibility for on-going training in the areas it is needed.

The future

In summer 1996, a WWW server was purchased, so that our catalogue can now be accessed on the Internet. The address is http://mikkel.scb.bibnet.dk/is/scb/dan/. With this Web site we have taken a big step into the future and already it has been useful for the other libraries Slagelse Central Library works with and for nearby educational institutions. The Internet opens up a whole new world not only for libraries but also for the arts, the information superhighway and human and institutional communication. The council's administrative network is open only to council employees. However, it is likely that, within a few years, the general public will be able, via the Internet, to access the council's home page and the information made available here. It seems probable that the library will be an important partner in this project.

Conclusions

Transition from one computer system to another cannot be planned carefully enough. Even though we considered ourselves to have been thorough, there have been many extra expenses as we have become aware of different requirements which were not in the system specification. More PCs and printers have been bought than were planned. More training has been necessary. The network proved not to be large enough, so this was increased and divided into two circuits (one for the administrative part which was linked to the town hall and one for the library system). The importance of staff training cannot be overestimated when implementing a new system and creating new job descriptions. One of the worst things that can happen is that manual routines are converted to the new system, thereby losing the advantages of more rational processes. Other libraries have had to pay for these electronic systems by reducing personnel. Slagelse Library has been spared this, but has felt obliged to use these more rational processes to better the service. In this respect, it is important to have imagination and an insight into the world of computers in order to see where improvements can be made.

7

Small is beautiful: migrating from SIMS to Heritage at Solihull Sixth Form College

Jan Condon

Introduction

Solihull Sixth Form College is a post-16 college incorporated since 1992 and belonging since then to the further education (FE) sector. It was established in 1974 by the local education authority (LEA) under school regulations to provide sixth form education for about 850 students at schools in the south of the Metropolitan Borough of Solihull in the West Midlands in purpose-built premises next to parkland.

At the time of writing, there are approximately 2240 students, the majority taking three 'A' level courses full-time, about 25% following GNVQ courses and with a wide offering of Open College Network courses providing enhancement to student programmes. There are a growing number of courses for adults.

The library was an integral feature of the original new building. The post of College Librarian was part of the academic establishment from the beginning of the College and provides the professional expertise to the library. Other posts are part-time, including a non-professional but experienced senior assistant and currently seven assistants, four of whom have extensive experience of library work in the public library sector. The number of staffing hours has increased from an original 46 hours in term time only to 4.5 full-time equivalent. In addition, since 1991, the network manager and IT assistants have been part of the Library and Learning Resources establishment.

The library inherited a core collection of 'A' level support texts from the six schools libraries whose sixth forms it replaced. Since then, it has always had a healthy annual budget and has also had access to capital project funds, both of which are subject to bidding processes. There is a stock of 22,000 items. CD-ROM has been a feature of the library since its introduction in 1988. There are also four IT Study Centres which give access to Microsoft products and curriculum software including CD-ROMs.

Access to stock originally took the form of a classified card catalogue and subject index, with a modified Browne issue system, often used in schools, using Gresswells issue cards. A part-time typist was employed to help with the production of the catalogue.

Automation history

Solihull Public Library short title catalogue

The college library does not have formal links with the service provided to the public by the Libraries and Arts Division of Solihull Education, Libraries and Arts Department, but in the past the then Solihull Public Library schools library service personnel attended meetings of schools librarians from the borough's secondary schools which included the College Librarian. The College Librarian developed contacts with public library staff, especially those at its Central Library which is a mere 20-minute walk from the College. Students were actively encouraged to use its services, their parents then being rate payers to the borough.

As a result of the proximity of the Central Library, it was thought that it would be a useful service development to give students access to the public library catalogue at the College. The public library cataloguing system in the late-1970s had been recently automated. With the cooperation of the Bibliographic Services Department and the borough's computer services, the system was examined to see if the same system could be used at the College or whether a union catalogue should be developed. Discussions took place with the bibliographic services librarian to explore possibilities. The short title catalogue was produced via the local authority computer services department. It was decided that, initially, the Sixth Form College Library and the FE College Library would make use of the same service and would get its catalogue produced on microfiches which would be exchanged so that both colleges and the public library service had notional local access to the stock. There were preliminary discussions on the feasibility of funding a direct link with the public library catalogue, in effect turning the Sixth Form College Library into a branch library for cataloguing and access to catalogues.

For a variety of reasons, these discussions were inconclusive. In the meantime, the advantages of using the system to produce and share fiches were many, including that

- resources across the borough and their locations could be made known to all college users
- micros were in their infancy and for schools were very expensive so could be viewed with interested caution
- library programs for small institutions were also at early stages of development so were not an option at that time.

In addition, the library no longer needed to rely on a secretary – who was more often than not needed to type UCCA forms and references for higher education and employment – for typing catalogue cards. And there was no filing!

Data input was taken from existing cards using agreed codes for the two college libraries and new stock was input in batch to produce annual fiches with quarterly updates. Fiches were produced in author, title and classified order. Added entries could be made using a code plus false stock number. A printout was provided for ease of checking and entries which did not meet the standard set by the forms used for data input were returned for reconsideration.

Students were instructed on the use of fiche catalogues and they used the Sixth Form College's own catalogue and that of the public library to locate materials needed. This system continued in use throughout the early- to mid-1980s.

Other IT applications

In the meantime, the BBC micro was in the ascendant in education. Some schools and commercial organizations wrote programs for cataloguing school libraries and these possibilities were often in the minds of school librarians. From the Sixth Form College's point of view, there would be insufficient computing power or storage capacity for the stock, which at that time was around 12,000 items. It was decided to stay with the short title catalogue, to continue to explore commercial database programs for cataloguing (there was a brief trial with a commercial package on a PC inherited from the office) and to provide BBC micros to provide word-processing for students to use in the library and as a means of using subject-specific software. We also tried out BBC database programmes such as SIR (Schools Information Retrieval)[1] and KWIRS (Key Words Information Retrieval System)[2] to produce resources lists and became involved with a British Library project accessing Data-Star and Profile with the addition of a modem to the BBC B.[3]

At that time, I was editor of *School Library Group news*, and in that capacity often was asked by school librarians about library automation (it was frequently assumed the library I managed had been automated in the full sense). Despite the power of the then 'mighty micro', I felt the time was not right for us to use it for automation. It was still a scarce resource which could be used in other educational ways. Indeed in the late-1980s when one of the main online databases used by the Sixth Form College, ECCTIS (Educational Counselling and Credit Transfer Information System)[4] became available on CD-ROM via a 286 PC and external CD-ROM drive, this service too was introduced, soon to be followed by an early version of the Grolier Encyclopedia. These services were quite deliberately explored, some may say at the expense of automation. Using databases of a more limited kind directly developed the skills and awareness of library staff and library users. At the same time, increased familiarity with large databases online gave an idea of what could be possible. It was apparent that computing power was increasing rapidly and that the spread of PCs and growth of networks in schools would be likely to have an effect on any future developments.

Implementation of SIMS

When the public library service decided to move to BLCMP, the Sixth Form College stayed with the short title catalogue – costs would have been prohibitive to have attempted to follow the same route.

Local management of schools (LMS) produced an incentive for companies to develop management information systems (MIS) for schools, some of which included a library management package or modules. Library packages were surveyed in a publication[5] from the then Central London Polytechnic, which provided a useful guide into what to look for when considering automation. Solihull schools decided to opt for SIMS (Schools Information Management System), which had developed directly from schools' experience. The LEA held demonstrations of SIMSLIBRARY for all those with responsibility for school libraries (the Sixth Form College was, at the time, operating under schools regulations).

SIMSLIBRARY offered a circulation as well as cataloguing system. Hands-on sessions were also arranged before decisions taken to opt in. The library staff had some reservations, largely based around the fact that data would have to be re-entered (there was no direct conversion program), and doubts about the ability of the system to cope with stock which was much larger and diverse in form than that of schools. Other drawbacks with SIMS were that on-screen messages were designed for younger school children as opposed to older students, and there would no longer be any link with the public library system or the FE College.

On balance, however, the library decided to join in the scheme as advantages of SIMSLIBRARY were felt to outweigh these drawbacks, in that

- there was support from the LEA
- there was technical support locally
- it was part of a suite of programs for MIS in schools – student data could be imported
- most of the feeder schools were using it, therefore there was every likelihood that students would be familiar with it.

A three-year programme of introducing SIMSLIBRARY was devised to tie in with the stock editing programme cycle, starting with the inputting of data (and broad keywords) for areas of stock most heavily used (history and English), and at the same time collecting data from items as they were borrowed/returned. In effect, this meant running a near double form of issue system to phase the new system in and the old one out.

The circulation system, therefore, temporarily comprised

1 student signs book card
2 book card used to enter brief details (accession, author and brief title) onto SIMSLIBRARY
3 book card filed by date due for return
4 book trapped on return
5 additional details added to SIMSLIBRARY from book

6 book card destroyed.
7 book marked 'S' denoting it had been added.

All new stock was added as purchased – keywords were allocated according to broad curriculum area and potential curriculum use. Student data was imported from STAR so that the circulation module could be used from the beginning. A data export program (Libtools) to enable us to take data from *Bookbank* was also used. Staff thought that it was somewhat unwieldy and, as keywords did not necessarily conform to what was appropriate for student use, after about six months' use it was abandoned in favour of direct input from the book itself.

The library had a range of 'non-book' resources for which SIMSLIBRARY allowed the system manager to detail a materials type code. This field by itself was not searchable, so the author field and keyword facility was also used to express material type.

The ISBN field allowed automatic input of data from the first copy for multiple copies – an important function as the library bought up to three copies of key texts and administered small class sets of books for departmental projects (up to 12 copies of the same title). Unfortunately, European ISBNs were not accepted, which was a drawback when cataloguing multiple copies of foreign language readers.

The Sixth Form College became incorporated as part of the FE sector in 1992 and started to expand considerably. As the stock grew in size and diversity of material, more data was added (the card catalogue was phased out in 1994). It became apparent that the system too would have to develop to keep up with need. Difficulty was experienced with keywords – those most frequently used could not be used in searches because there were too many items. The system was not sufficiently flexible to allow for added or analytical entries (e.g. in the case of collections of plays or part items, which was particularly awkward as there was a growing theatre studies course). Although there was an owner field, there was no location field. As stock was often deposited with the library by departments who retained ownership and might need a searchable owner and location entry, this would be a problem which could become a major drawback if proposed learning centres developed. An update did give an optional notes field which proved useful to staff but less use for OPAC users where it was not offered as an expansion of information found. The length of fields too became a problem where items such as off-prints or audiovisual items had lengthy titles or authors names (e.g. corporate authors). In addition, there was no interface between SIMSLIBRARY and FMS, the finance module. This meant that order data had to be entered on both parts of the system from the keyboard. As far as the user database was concerned, the system had difficulties with students with non-school type leaving dates (short courses, evening courses). Although there was a strong user group and a development programme for SIMSLIBRARY, library staff were not sure that the package would develop to suit a rapidly growing and diverse population of users in the immediate future.

Lessons learned from the short title catalogue and SIMSLIBRARY experience

- Whatever system is in place, it should be capable of expansion to meet different kinds of user and to cope with different, often multiple, types of materials resources.
- It is better to phase in a new system than to convert at one go, not only so that problems can be smoothed out but also so that library staff become familiar with the new system.
- It can be confusing to users to have more than one kind of catalogue, so the phasing-in should have a short and defined timescale.
- The system had to suit the needs of the Sixth Form College, which may be different from those of other organizations (e.g. schools).
- Consultation with the staff who would be responsible for the day-to-day use of the system brought good ideas for practical implementation as well as for the selection of a system.
- An IT specialist (the network manager) could offer a different and useful perspective on a system.
- An outside view (KPMG) could influence the future direction taken.

Selection of a new system

At the end of 1994, an outline specification for a replacement system which would be acceptable was produced.

The specification included

- the conversion of existing data by the system provider
- compatibility with existing equipment
- the ability to link to other systems (data import) including *BNB*, *Bookbank*, SIMS student data (STAR)
- a user-friendly OPAC with all fields searchable
- easy access to authority files
- the ability to cope with multimedia or multi/mixed material resources
- the ability to cope with analytical entries for plays, part works and serials
- the ability to cope with infinite number of keywords
- that all fields be searchable
- an acquisitions module with the capacity to produce financial data
- a serials package
- extensive fields for data entry to cope with long titles/corporate authors
- the ability to cope with different kinds of users (e.g. leaving dates and alerts for one-year courses, short courses, temporary personnel and full addresses)
- on-site training as an option
- a good record of support.

Further information was collected from companies producing library systems, exhibitions and conference stands were visited to get a feel for what was on the market and other librarians were consulted. Two systems, ALICE and Heritage, emerged as front runners. In addition, the library staff, including the network manager, had an opportunity to comment on the existing system and to state what they wanted from a system. Then the specification was revised.

A little later, the Sixth Form College commissioned a review of its management information systems, including the library system, from KPMG Management Consulting. KPMG advised the library not to tie itself into the Sixth Form College's MIS for the sake of it, and accepted the specification drawn up. The introduction of a new system formed part of the library development plan and was taken forward into the College's operating statements and action plans.

In addition to the criteria listed in the specification, any replacement system had to be realistically affordable via the bidding process, to have excellent support services with an active user group, and, preferably, be developed by the company selling it so that the sales staff had a vested interest in its success. The user group structure and company support were of paramount importance, as there was no longer a local authority support system as the Sixth Form College, like other sixth form and FE colleges, was no longer funded locally. On the other hand, unlike previously, there was technical support on site in the form of a network manager and administrator. Also, as a result of previous experience with SIMSLIBRARY and an increasing stock of CD-ROM databases, library staff were used to carrying out activities using computers.

Instead of relying on demonstrations and information provided by companies in the market, a less orthodox approach was adopted. Before the funding bid was finalized, a telephone survey was carried out to local libraries and to those colleagues in the School Library Group of The Library Association (SLG) and The Library Association's Colleges of Higher and Further Education Group (CoHFE), whose professional judgment and practical experience was rated highly enough for them to 'tell it as it was'! This apparently unscientific approach proved to be exceptionally useful.

The following two questions were asked:

1 What system do you have and what do you think of it?
2 If you could choose a new system, what would it be and why?

Colleagues gave full and frank replies! Heritage from Inheritance Systems[6] emerged as a firm favourite with its excellent, caring support service being cited as a major strength, in addition to its flexibility and ease of use for library staff and users. This, together with the fact that modules were comparatively inexpensive and could be added 'as and when'. Moreover, the company could convert data from SIMSLIBRARY and would provide on-site training.

To double check, in order to remind everyone about the system's various facets and to check what the two senior library assistants and network manager thought of it, a second demonstration was arranged before the final bid went forward. At the second demonstration, Heritage was approved unanimously by the assistants and network manager. The bid was successful and an order placed in November 1996.

Installation of the new system

As the work of the library had grown, it was decided that as well as a change of library management system, the opportunity would be taken to barcode the stock. This task would run alongside a major stock edit of all stock so that only that which it was thought would be needed would be retained, barcoded and appear on the Heritage system. The edit would take place during the spring term, but as teaching staff were usually invited into this process, withdrawn stock was to be retained in store until the end of the academic year when they would have time to review it. A timetable for implementation of Heritage was drawn up. It was decided that it made more sense to start an academic year with a new system from the library users' point of view but, because a large number of users would be on block leave before their examinations in the second part of the summer term, a phased introduction might be possible. In addition, the timescale would allow for the carrying out of the stock edit/barcoding and for the training of staff so that everyone was familiar and comfortable with the system by the end of the summer holiday. In addition, there was sufficient time for new hardware, including a new server needed for the administration work of the College, regardless of Heritage, to be in place and all modules to be tested in the field. There should also be sufficient time to check out the data conversion from SIMSLIBRARY to Heritage and to clean up any errors in data entry made in the past.

The library system is currently hosted on the college administration server. The network manager advised that it should be kept there for data security although sufficient access has been bought to launch the catalogue on the student network server, always the original intention. Further network issues will be reviewed next year.

At the time of writing the stock surveys are well underway and Heritage has been installed on a standalone PC in the library workroom. As Heritage has a dummy library database available, this will be used for familiarization sessions for all of the library staff. The intention is by the time of block leave, to have Heritage networked in place for use by the rising second year students and to leave SIMSLIBRARY operating on a standalone to provide the service for those students who will leave at the end of the academic year. Most new items will have been added to stock by May from the current buying round and anything received after data is converted will be added to Heritage only. The timescale also allows for the development of any changes in routines and new induction materials to take place in good time for the new academic year, including the testing of data transfer from STAR, the SIMS module containing student data, to Heritage.

Human issues

Consultation

Working as the sole professional librarian in an organization is a scenario common to many college and most school librarians. The informal networks which develop are extremely valuable and, although opinion (and experience) may be considered as soft data compared with more usual methods of cost benefit or SWOT analysis, when given by respected colleagues who have nothing to gain by giving that opinion, the information obtained is invaluable.

Consulting others within the institution is also important. Many are too polite to complain about the catalogue or see it as an administrative issue, so no wholesale questionnaire to assess users' opinions was issued. Instead use was simply observed. There will be guidance on using the new system circulated to existing staff and students in the summer term and to new staff and students as part of induction in the autumn.

Library staff

Library staff, on the other hand, are using many aspects of a system every day of their working lives. Two strategies were adopted here.

First, an in-service training day was used to get all staff involved in the process of change.

Using flip charts, in groups of two or three, staff brainstormed what they liked about the existing system and what they did not. The whole group then discussed the issues raised and noted down what they would expect of any new system. This discussion took place in advance of the specification being finalized and raised additional issues such as that of short courses and locations of materials not in the main library; comments were also made on the problems of much-used keywords and how users might be more dependent on staff if the catalogue informed them that an enquiry was too difficult because of the 'overworked' keywords. At this stage too, practical implementation, including barcoding issues were discussed.

The second strategy was to involve the senior assistants in the final look at the preferred system before making a final decision. At this stage, had anything been identified as a major drawback, other candidates would have been reconsidered. The senior assistants are not only experienced users but also help to train new staff and are those who most often staff the help desk to assist students.

The involvement of all staff should help to make the migration to the new system easier.

IT staff

When the short title catalogue was introduced, the technical processes were in the hands of the local authority computing department. When SIMSLIBRARY was introduced, installation was carried out by an LEA team with some support from an IT teacher. Now that the Sixth Form College has its own networks and network manager, it has responsibility for the system and migration to it, with the support of the new supplier. Currently the IT network manager and assistant are part of the Library and Learning Resources team and this has meant that the manager has been involved and consulted throughout the whole process, contributing the technical know-how lacked by the librarian.

Library users

It is anticipated that users will soon adapt to any new system! (About 50% of college users change at least annually.) Current partner schools have SIMSLIBRARY and ALICE, but students come from an increasingly wider area and have experience of a number of different systems. Heritage has a new Windows-based OPAC, which may well prove more popular than the older DOS one. It is also hoped to scan the library plan into the system so that locating items will be even easier. Paper-based support will be developed and users kept informed during the implementation process by announcements in the College bulletin and on notice boards.

College administration

The Head of Administration has been consulted during the process to date and links with the students database (STAR) will be maintained. As the finance system has no existing automated links to the library system, any involvement with it will be caused by changes in ordering systems because of the new acquisitions module and online ordering which is currently being piloted.

Training

Familiarization is the first phase. All staff are to be given time to explore the new system by being given exercises and case studies to use on dummy data. These materials are being developed in-house, but using the excellent and dauntingly comprehensive manual provided as guidance.

One day's training on site has been bought and will take place after the transfer of data so that staff can transfer the experience gained on the dummy data to the actual data. This experience is expected to influence the design of materials for use with library users.

Conclusions

Moving from SIMSLIBRARY to Heritage is already a very different experience from that of converting to SIMSLIBRARY from a centrally managed system. It can be summed up in Table 7.1.

Table 7.1

To SIMSLIBRARY	To Heritage
No previous experience of PCs	All staff confident in using PCs
No direct prior experience of direct data input	All staff have taken part in data input
Data needed manual conversion	Most data should be converted by Inheritance
Technical support from LEA	Technical support from college staff
Purchased via LEA	Purchased via college funds
Users unfamiliar with OPACs	Users familiar with computers including OPACs
Long timespan to edit and convert data	Data conversion and stock edit to take place within two terms

It is highly unlikely that whatever systems are chosen they will fulfil all criteria for all time! Developments both technical and educational are likely constantly to present new possibilities and new demands. Learning to be as flexible as the system will allow is an important lesson.

The need for the systems manager to take time out from any other work – invariably difficult in the case of school and college personnel – is essential at an early stage after any formal training so that he or she becomes thoroughly familiar with the system. It is a crucial task if all aspects are to be fully exploited. In some cases a more difficult problem to be faced than 'technofear' and lack of time is quite simply a dislike of cataloguing!

The importance of the views of others, of the different interests, experience or angles immediate colleagues present, should not be underestimated. One of the best experiences was having to explain what was needed to a management consultant, who knew little about library systems. Talking to librarians in other colleges too was an essential exercise and has provided an introduction to existing users for future help and advice. For library systems where there is only one professional librarian, self-discipline to keep to a timetable and also to be flexible, self confidence that the right choices have been made and can be acted upon and, perhaps most importantly, using people networks to help make decisions are of vital importance. No one is alone!

References

1 Schools Information Retrieval software developed from a British Library project. See Rowbottom, M. E., Payne, A. W. and Cronin, B., *The schools information retrieval (SIR) project*, British Library, 1983 (Library and information research report; 15).

2 Key Words Information Retrieval System (KWIRS) was written by Norman Paton and used in the MISLIP Project. See Williams, D., Herring, J. E. and Bain, L. M., *The microcomputer in the school library project (MISLIP)*,

Aberdeen, Robert Gordon Institute of Technology, 1986.

3 Irving, A., *Wider horizons: online information services in schools*, British Library, 1990 (Library and Information Research Report; 80).

4 ECCTIS on CD-ROM is produced by ECCTIS 2000, the UK courses information service.

5 Leeves, J. and Manson, A., *Guide to library systems for schools*, London, Polytechnic of Central London, 1989.

6 Inheritance Systems, Newtec Place, Magdalen Road, Oxford.

8 A tale of two systems

Barry Hickman and Steve Penn

Part 1: the customer's perspective
Barry Hickman

Setting the stage

Coventry City Libraries is a local authority-provided public library service to Coventry, a city in the heartland of England. It serves an urban population of 303,000 with one central library, 11 static service points (neighbourhood libraries) and a mobile library. There is also a community library based in a school and a hospital library service which serves the staff and patients in the city's largest hospital. Although both of these are offline in computerized circulation terms, their stock is still added to the library catalogue. There are plans to put the community library online in the very near future, with a feasibility study due to take place within the next year to examine the issues involved in putting the hospital library service online at a later date. The mobile library uses a notebook PC purely to capture transactions, the data from which is downloaded to the main system at the end of each day.

The library service serves a population drawn from diverse cultural backgrounds and provides a wide range of library materials from all its service points. The Central Library is situated in the main traffic-free shopping area in the city centre and occupies a large converted ballroom on two floors (surely one of few libraries to have had Led Zeppelin and The Rolling Stones playing live on the main floor). The neighbourhood libraries, like so many urban library systems, are diverse in character, ranging from an ex-RAF wooden hut (a 'temporary' structure built in the 1930s) through Carnegie libraries to more modern purpose-built structures dating from the 1960s.

The library service forms part of the Cultural Services Division within the Leisure Services Department. The staffing structure is based on three service divisions: Central and Special Services (which covers the Central Library public services, the Tourist Information Centre, Multicultural Services, Schools Library Service and the Hospital Library); Local Services (which comprises 12 local libraries based on six neighbourhoods) and Management and Support Services (which is responsible for the technical, bibliographical and administrative functions).

Automation history

Development towards an automated library management system has followed similar lines to many other public library authorities. From the nostalgic Browne system a change to photocharging was made, and while operating this system, the first steps towards computerization were taken. In 1970, the catalogue was input to the Council's mainframe, laying the foundation for future developments.

Plessey's computerized issue system went live in Coventry in September 1976, linked to the bibliographic and borrower databases on the mainframe cataloguing system. Although this was a step forward in terms of stock control, the front end and its processor constituted a very simple number-crunching system. Automated reservations and overdue notice production (albeit with the delays associated with an offline system) at the time were viewed by library staff as a very real step forward in automating processes which until then had been particularly staff intensive. The Central Library, the 11 branches and the mobile library all operated through the Plessey system. Life revolved around the magnetic tape (floppies were not invented) and the mainframe until October 1985.

The hunt for a new, fully integrated online system started in 1983. It was specified that the new system must be operated jointly with the then Lanchester Polytechnic Library, so that one system could run both libraries, a decision embracing various political, financial and other considerations. The process of getting two very different library services, with their diverse and sometimes diametrically opposed requirements, to agree on a single system took a great deal of work and cooperation on both sides. Very late in the day, and very near a decision, a US company called Computerized Library Systems International (CLSI) asked for their system (LIBS 100) to be considered for the contract, which it eventually won at tender. At this time, CLSI had no systems running outside the USA, but despite this they won the contract to automate Coventry. Thus began a very unhappy period for Coventry's library staff – the single system centre for both libraries was located in the Polytechnic Library building and implementation timescales were condensed because the City Central Library sites were relocating to a new site (in the converted ballroom). That, alongside the fact that CLSI had not only grossly undersized the system but also could not get the separate processors to talk to each other, led to a very messy 12 months. In fact, the Polytechnic and the public library never did operate on a joint system (the Polytechnic was relieved to operate as a separate system on its own processor). For several months the Central Library was on one processor while the branch libraries were on another and for some processes response times could be measured in minutes rather than seconds. Eventually, the many problems were overcome, legal action avoided and LIBS 100 went on to be a very good reliable system, but it had taken two years in computer hell to achieve. As a company CLSI, or 'Sleazy' as we knew them (they always preferred 'Classy'), were excellent both in their support structure and the staff involved, providing a service which is unlikely will ever to be matched again.

Owing to financial restrictions, Coventry became time-locked on a certain release of software in 1989, and despite various attempts to upgrade, one of which even involved the construction of a new system centre in the Central Library, version 27.45 of LIBS 100 was to be retained until it was eventually turned off in 1995. In 1992, CLSI were taken over by Geac, once again prompting a search for ways of introducing a new system. In 1993, a window of opportunity opened in the political and financial situation in Coventry which gave us the opportunity to go ahead and search for a new system. There would be no new money available, so anything we did would have to be financed from within current resources.

Which system?

Over the years, we had gained a lot of experience of what goes wrong with computer systems and how not to implement a new one, so this time we were determined not to relive those mistakes. There was a recognition, however, that new mistakes would be made, but, for sanity's sake and the fact that the staff would have caused actual bodily harm if things went wrong with this implementation, there was a determination to take as much time as was needed for the process of specifying and selecting a new system, and get it as right as possible – first time. Realistically, we knew that it would probably take as much as two years between starting out and going live, which as it turned out was exactly right.

Three members of staff were involved in the selection process throughout, with others to be involved as required. Bob Sidney (Principal Assistant City Librarian – a strange title as there ceased to be a City Librarian some years previously) was there to take responsibility for the project, Barry Hickman (Systems Librarian) looked after all the technicalities and Marie Smart (Bibliographical Services Librarian) tended to all the bibliographical conversion issues and acted as a steadying influence on the other two.

A search of the literature and a look at such system specifications as could be obtained at that time did not turn up much useful information. We determined to write a new specification from scratch and, having decided that realistically it could be done in six months, an extended target of 12 months was set so that it would be as near to perfect as possible. Having discussed ideas of how to pitch the specification, we decided to describe in detail every item of functionality required from the new system and have the system vendors respond line-by-line on how their product would or would not fulfil each requirement. We acknowledged the fact that no single system would be able to supply exactly what we wanted and the evaluation process had to be tailored to accommodate that fact and to provide the system which most closely matched or promised to match our perceived needs, as expressed in the specification.

While in the process of writing the specification, we invited a selection of six suppliers to demonstrate their products to a team of staff drawn from all levels within the library service. At an early stage we realized that the manager's view of what we needed and the view of counter staff could be quite different, and that if the staff as a whole were to 'own' the new system, input should be accepted from anyone who wished to voice an opinion. Our selected suppliers were those which were considered most likely to tender for the contract at the end of the day. System demonstrations are hard work, can be very boring and, to be honest, were unlikely to sway our opinions one way or another anyway. We used this process to look at the market place, see what was on offer, and weave the good (and bad) bits of what was on offer into the specification. This stage was hard work and unexpectedly confusing when trying to remember which of the products did what and in what way. However, it did raise awareness and provide a much clearer view of what might be bought in the end. It also served to clear away any staff misconceptions and prejudices. By the time we reached the tendering process, we had a completely open mind on who would provide the new system.

The specification was drafted and given to the whole staff for their comments. A huge amount of constructive comment was received, all of which was answered individually and put into the specification before rereleasing it for further comment. This time very little needed to be amended. After the necessary checking for inconsistencies and the tidying-up process, the finished article was handed over to the City Supplies Division to handle the cross-European tendering process. It was decided not to charge for the specification document and was also made available on floppy disk so that companies could use it to formulate their response to tender documents as required. During the three months taken to complete the tender process, the methods for evaluating the bids and for arriving at a final choice were finalized.

It was necessary to have a completely impartial way of evaluating the tender documents when they arrived. We decided to apply the same equal opportunity principles as those used in selecting staff through the interview process. Each area of functionality was weighted, giving a count of 1 for those areas of least importance (e.g. serials control), through to a count of 3 for important modules (e.g. circulation). Thus, less important areas of functionality could not unduly tip the balance when scoring and more important areas of functionality would score more highly. A scoring document was drawn up giving one line to each one of the detailed items of functionality in the specification.

Each item of functionality was scored from the 'Response to tender' document for each system on the following basis.

0 = Not mentioned, no response.
1 = Promised at a long-term, later date.
2 = Promised within 12 months.
3 = Functionality partially present.
4 = Functionality existing, but not quite as requested.
5 = Functionality as requested.

Hence, each detail in the response to tender would be marked then multiplied by the weighting applied to the module concerned to arrive at a final score. The only areas open to human interpretation would be scores 3 and 4, but we felt that, with three individuals carrying out the marking process, consistency would be maintained. In the event of two systems scoring closely, the final winner would be determined through further contact with the bidders involved. A factor to be taken into account at a later stage was affordability, because there was only a finite amount of capital money to spend and work would have to be kept within revenue budgets. If one system scored highly but was too expensive, then post-tender negotiations would be used to reach an agreement or some functionality would have to be sacrifice for the sake of affordability. If two systems scored similarly and cost a similar amount of money, then further demonstrations would be requested in front of a panel of staff which would decide which system was the most suitable.

The specification had set out broadly how costs should be presented, but we suspected that the way different companies would present their costing details could cloud the issue when looking at the initial outlay and projected running costs. Detailed analysis and further contact with the vendors involved was deemed to make this manageable. From 12 tender documents sent out, five completed responses were received by the appointed date. Interestingly, one of the systems reviewed at the demonstration stage did not tender and one system which had not been reviewed did submit a response. Again, no timescale was set between receipt of tender and entry into contract negotiations with the nominated supplier, as it was suspected that this could be quite long and drawn out depending on the result of the scoring and financial analysis. Added to this would be the time taken for company searches, etc., prior to informing the winner.

Needless to say, one of the companies who submitted a tender did not present it in the format specified and preferred to submit instead a standard 'off the shelf' tender. The initial response was to disallow the tender and the problems of marking it, however, it was put to one side while the rest were marked and returned to last of all. Each of the tenders took a whole day to mark, with the 'off the shelf' example taking two days of hard work to extract the necessary information. Once all the scores for each system were entered into a spreadsheet, the result was one which had not been envisaged: the same company (BLCMP) won the day both on functionality and on price – and came within the capital and revenue budgets. It was a quick and relatively painless end to what could have been a frustrating round of post-tender negotiations with a number of companies.

At this stage the library service made an error of judgment. Staff were told that the BLCMP's Talis system had been chosen, but they were also asked not to tell anyone until the company searches had been carried out and until BLCMP had been informed officially. The timing was quite unfortunate. The 1994 Library Resources Exhibition took place at the National Exhibition Centre a few days later, at which Coventry staff inundated BLCMP's stand giving the game away completely!

Talis was to be implemented on 3 April 1995 so that its introduction would fit nicely into the financial and circulation year. (1 April was avoided for obvious reasons.) That timescale allowed four months to tidy up the contract and six months to complete the installation and implementation. Wrong again! The contractual negotiations because of various factors took until early December 1994 and the 'go live' date was moved to early July to compensate. Unfortunately, Geac had already been served with notice of our intent to dispense with their services at the end of March 1995, and the cost of extending their cover for our LIBS system to the projected 'go live' date did not represent good value for money. Over the years of looking after LIBS 100, I had gained a lot of experience in coaxing our ageing PDP hardware to perform as advertised, so we decided to operate without maintenance cover from Geac for the 14 weeks between April and 'go live' in July. Those 14 weeks actually became 18 weeks in reality, but our risk management (called in some circles 'mad gamble') paid off and the PDPs chugged on until they were eventually turned off in August 1995. Had something gone wrong, then there would have been penalty prices to pay for repairs.

Installing Talis

Having had such a depressing experience while migrating to LIBS 100, we were determined that the change to Talis would not follow the same disastrous course and that this time everything would be checked and double checked in fine detail. The previous mistakes would not be allowed to happen again. Being aware that a new set of problems would take their place, the crystal ball was dusted off to try to predict them. On the one hand, the project could not be rushed, having decided that if more time was required the 'go live' date could easily be moved. On the other hand, the old system was running on borrowed time and any extension of the time taken to implement Talis would mean an increased likelihood of LIBS giving up the ghost.

The same three individuals who drove the selection process also drove the installation phase of the project and, in the most part, dispensed with their other responsibilities to dedicate a majority of their working hours to the implementation. On the practical side, a technical assistant had been appointed and, during the period of the selection process had been keeping LIBS running in order to release the Systems Librarian's time. Other staff with specialist knowledge were sucked into the project on an 'as required' basis.

The change to Talis had to be done on the 'big bang' principle. The LIBS system was running from a system centre in what had become Coventry University, while Talis would be operated from the new system centre in the Central Library. We were bringing forward our existing peripherals to work with Talis and were also intending to reuse our existing communications equipment (purely because we could not afford the expense of changing or upgrading them). The Talis configuration had been sized for 128 concurrent users (48 more than on LIBS) to allow for future expansion and a bit extra to allow for the unknown. Staff were asked where they needed extra terminals, which until now had been impossible to provide (because LIBS did not have a single spare port) and the laying in the cables for these terminals began as soon as possible. Contractors laid in an ethernet spine within the Central Library and the new system centre to which existing and new hardwires would link via a number of terminal servers. In the Central Library, three 8-channel multiplexors were replaced by three 16-channel term servers. These were a direct replacement for existing kit as there was no desire to increase the workloads by wholesale replacement of the existing hardwired infrastructure.

The existing communications equipment consisted of 'vintage 1985' multi-plexors running with slightly newer 9600 baud modems over dedicated BT data lines. These were moved from the University system centre to the Central Library at the last possible moment before going live and were reused with Talis. The main concern with this equipment was whether it would actually work quickly enough for Talis to be successfully implemented into the neigh-bourhood libraries. We knew that the Central Library would be okay as its peripherals plugged directly into terminal servers on the main ethernet spine, so at least the busiest and largest service point would work successfully. Exhaustive enquiries were made of the equipment manufacturers but no one could say whether the data throughput was going to be sufficient to allow Talis to work. A number of tests were run in-house which proved that the equipment would actually display Talis on a remote terminal, but for various reasons it was not possible to simulate a multiterminal, busy library environment. We were about 80% confident that this equipment would work and laid the problem aside to be addressed with some urgency after 'go live' if necessary.

We shunned the 'modern' trend away from dumb terminals preferring instead to carry on using them, first on the grounds of cost and second on the grounds of simplicity – we had already found that PCs linked to a network can pose some complications both in terms of staff usage and support. Since all of the peripherals would be supported in-house by the Systems Librarian and the staff were already used to dumb terminals, now was not a good time to change.

Tests and confirmation of setups on existing peripherals was carried out by BLCMP and, at a later point, by ourselves when the system centre hardware was in place at Central Library. The only major problem encountered was that screen printing was impossible to accomplish with any existing terminals. Having determined to increase the terminal population upon implementation, BLCMP was asked which type of new terminal should be purchased bearing in mind the need to be able to print out data from the system. At this stage, an unfortunate communications glitch took place. The sales and implementation side of BLCMP were advised by their technical staff that the Data General DG414 would be their recommended terminal in future. Unfortunately, the 'techies' did not tell the sales staff that a problem with printing from these ter-minals had already been discovered and that the Wyse 520 should be the ter-minal to be used in future. Needless to say, the library service went on to buy

25 DG414s, which it soon discovered would not perform as required. BLCMP resolved the problem by lending us Wyse 520 terminals for the period between 'go live' and a date in the near future when full data subset printing would become available on Talis.

The City Library Service had been used to operating independently of existing computing support within the City Council ever since the installation of LIBS back in 1985. On installing a specialist turnkey system, the City Library had moved deliberately away from the mainframe concept which in 1985 was running 99% of computing applications across the Council. Employing a specialist member of staff in the form of a Systems Librarian, meant that all support and contractual issues had been handled in-house without reference to the outside world. The library service's expertise had grown and no one else had any understanding of its system software or indeed of its hardware platform or peripherals. Although we had operated in relative isolation from the rest of the City Council, at the time of selecting a new system it was decided that some use be made of the computing expertise which existed 'out there'. Fortunately, there was a great deal of expert help with contractual negotiations and hardware acceptance testing, but apart from these two areas we were unable to call on help from elsewhere – librarians make mysterious demands on computer systems!

Having used an in-house system for almost nine years, our database was well-developed and had quite a few useful touches built in which we did not want to lose, such as a very good subject approach. Under LIBS, comprehensive use of SCATs (statistical categories) had been made, whereby a numeric value represented a particular type of item, and for borrowers, age, gender, cultural background and language requirements. This enabled a reasonable level of statistical analysis of transactions. *All* of the existing bibliographic and borrower data needed to be carried forward to Talis. A major problem would be that the LIBS system was non-MARC and there would have to be a conversion to a MARC format with our only member of staff with any recent experience in MARC cataloguing having just returned home to Brazil. It was with some trepidation that the library service approached the series of meetings which would determine how the LIBS database would be converted for use under Talis.

Converting the stock

Luckily two of the staff leading the implementation had cataloguing expertise, Marie Smart as Bibliographical Services Officer and Bob Sidney who in a previous reincarnation had been Marie's predecessor. The Systems Librarian, although a lapsed librarian, had little understanding of the 'black arts' of AACR, cataloguing and such like.

It was difficult to envisage how the local fields from the LIBS database would fit into Talis's MARC format, and, in particular how they could be displayed in a useful and meaningful way for the staff and public to use in the OPAC. Staff felt uncomfortable to be so technically unaware, however, as time and discussions with BLCMP's analysts progressed, comfort returned and we found ourselves referring to MARC tags quite naturally. By the time a conversion strategy had been agreed upon, it had dawned on BLCMP that this would be no easy conversion though when documented it had looked simplicity itself! We all feel with hindsight that given our time over again we would do it differently, because in retrospect, the converted data has presented some problems, but we are also sure that we did the best possible job at the time. I must also add that even now we are still not really sure of quite how we would have made a better job of handling the conversion. So be warned that local data converted from one system to another carries with it inherent problems and just doesn't fit into the new system in quite the same way (bibliothecarii caveant!)

The intention here is not to give a blow-by-blow account of which field converted to which tag, or indeed which item field was converted to where, as this would most likely induce sleep for even the worst insomniac. The conversion (non-MARC LIBS to Talis) was unique, so further discussion of the fine detail would serve little purpose in this context, and could fill a weighty tome in its own right.

From the technical point of view, a few snags were encountered. The LIBS system had the ability to dump its database to tape, albeit the prehistoric half-inch magnetic tape variety. This had been done several times previously in order to prepare masters for microfiche catalogue production and knowing that the database fitted onto 20 spools of tape and each tape took 15 hours to fill, meant that there should be no problem. Wrong again. There had never been an attempt to dump every field from a catalogue record complete with every field from the attached item fields. By the time testing of this dump began, there were only days before the severing of the contract with Geac. The manual which purported to lay out exactly how the data would be written to tape and indeed just how this process might be accomplished did not seem to be complete. Alternatively, the fact that it was written in US English could have led us astray. All of the ex-CLSI employees who would have been able to offer expert support in this field had long since left Geac, so we were left out on a limb. Geac were asked if we could pay them to run the dump from one of our back-up sets, but they did not have nor could they lash up a PDP system on which to do it, such was their spares holding. As luck would have it, however, BLCMP's Sales Manager had previously run a LIBS system and had later worked for CLSI, so could remember quite a lot about the mysteries of dumping data to tape. After several false starts and a lot of tinkering, LIBS was finally persuaded to give over its secrets to magnetic tape. It had become obvious during testing that more than 20 tapes were going to be needed for bibliographical data, and then yet more for the borrower database. At this time, I made what was to become the single most frustrating error of the whole implementation. I borrowed ten reels of tape from our mainframe computer department instead of buying new ones. All but one of these reels was to fail during the various dumps causing the library service and BLCMP untold hours of extra work recreating tapes and deleting duplicated data, before ending up with a complete dump of the LIBS bibliographic data on a machine in Birmingham ready for conversion. We didn't start dumping to tape early enough, having underestimated the problems that might be encountered. When the dumping did start, the suspect tapes caused delay and this phase alone served to put the whole project behind schedule.

By the time the conversion was under way, the Talis system was up and running in the new system centre at Central Library, and LIBS was still running from the system centre at the University. Several terminals in Central Library were running Talis for the purpose of setting up parameters, training and testing various parts of the software. It was agreed that for testing the conversion a subset of a couple of hundred records would be accepted, to make sure that all the old data had converted correctly. We were able to call up the same record on LIBS and Talis and compare them to check the conversion per the agreed documentation. As expected, this phase of the operation took several weeks to accomplish successfully, but eventually everything seemed to be converting to the correct fields in the Talis records. Having completed the title load, the items were to be added as a separate process. For a variety of reasons the process that loaded items into the database refused to work correctly – frustrating all attempts to complete the tapes to enable the bibliographic database to be in place by early June 1995. The Bibliographical Services Section was to 'go live' on 12 June 1995, but that date came and went and still the set of tapes had not arrived. There was a delay of several days while the converted tapes were prepared by BLCMP, which was quite understandably a time-consuming process given the size of the database. Loading of tapes began on 15 June 1995 and finished ten days later, after much hard work to complete the process in the shortest possible time. The very first item tape caused some consternation in the way in which it loaded, but the problem was laid to rest and the process continued. Little did we know however that this first tape problem would haunt us until October 1996 because it had introduced some duplicate barcode numbers into the system. Suffice it to say that having had some 5500 duplicate barcodes in the system caused all sorts of difficulties for the staff using and managing it. In October 1996, the duplicates were identified and removed.

In retrospect, more time should have been taken to check in greater detail, but by the time the conversion was working correctly, time was marching on towards the 'go live' date and we were heartily tired of the constant checking and reloading. On starting to use Talis, three problems were identified which had resulted from the conversion and which continued into the second year of running Talis. They were

1 duplicate control numbers
2 duplicate barcode numbers
3 sound recording bibliographic records which instead of relating to a single format (e.g. CD), actually had items in all three sound recording formats attached to them.

We have been working towards a resolution of all of these problems ever since.

The task of loading the bibliographic database proved to be not quite as laborious as dumping the old database to tape. Everybody was keen to get the database loaded as quickly as possible, so that any problems could be identified and overcome without adding further to the timescale.

Converting borrowers

Compared to the bibliographic conversion, the transfer of borrower data was comparatively easy. LIBS allowed the 'purging' of borrower data by a number of different criteria and only what we considered to be 'active' borrowers were taken forward to Talis. All borrowers who hadn't used the library in the last year were stripped out of the database, thus reducing it from a figure far in excess of the city population to 130,000. It may have been a little over-zealous, in that a considerable number of borrowers with existing tickets came to use the library only to find that they were no longer registered. Experience after the event showed that a more realistic figure would have been 18 months or perhaps two years, but at least there was the certainty that a great deal of 'dead wood' had been removed.

At no time had we contemplated converting the files containing borrower loans, feeling that this would be fraught with danger. Talis was started with a clean sheet and in effect threw away the LIBS loan records. However, there wasn't the option to discharge LIBS loans anyway, due to the wholesale movement of the communications cabinet from the University system. The old LIBS system would be completely isolated.

The LIBS borrower record contained a string of characters known as the Alternative Patron Identifier (APATID), which was used as an alternative way of searching the borrower database. The APATID was made up of the first three letters of the surname, first initial and date of birth but the only part of it that would be of use on Talis was the date of birth. The conversion extracted the date of birth and inserted it into the date of birth. field in the Talis record. Unfortunately, the APATIDs also contained some anomalies in the dates of birth (alphabetic characters) which were inserted by staff to deal with twins with the same initials, people who preferred not to give their date of birth, etc. These were not be converted to Talis but left blank so that staff could attempt to fill in a correct version at the time of re-registration. Where address data had not fitted the LIBS fields correctly, staff had been used to inserting data to fit as best they could, which was fine under LIBS, however as soon as a more rigid structure was imposed on the data, some of the records took on a very strange look, and some records acted very strangely under interrogation because of extra character spaces, etc. Again it was agreed that staff would put the records right at the time of each tri-annual re-registration, so that in theory by the time we had been running Talis for three years the borrower database would be corrected. Actually, the staff have made an excellent job of searching out the problems and correcting them, so even now at 18 months since going live, the database is generally very clean.

Two snags were encountered, which, had they not been so amusing, would have been very annoying. The first of these was a quirk of Sybase (the RDBMS used by Talis). On conversion, anyone born earlier than 1 January 1970 was given a date of birth of 01/01/70 – resulting in a borrower database with no one older than 25! BLCMP had kept a tape of borrower numbers and dates of birth, and a few weeks after going live the quirk was fixed and the data reinput from tape.

The second problem could not be fixed automatically, so will take a little longer to remove. Two types of barcode are used in Coventry, UK Plessey (12 digits) and CLSI Codabar (14 digits). The Plessey codes are prefixed with a letter 'D', so validation software to accommodate alphabetics in barcodes had to be produced by BLCMP. Unfortunately, in doing this, an intriguing problem was introduced. If while searching for a borrower by name and forename, that borrower's name just happened to start with a 'D' and was 12 character spaces long, including the comma and space (e.g. Duke, Adrian), the system reported that the borrower was not on file because it was looking for the name in the borrower barcode table! Already staff are making moves to wipe out Plessey borrower barcodes, and when this is complete, BLCMP will remove that part of the validation software and with it the problem.

Going live

After many weeks of preparation, the time for the change from CLSI to Talis finally arrived. We intended to make the move over one weekend and to be ready to start using the new system on Monday in Central Library, and on Wednesday in the local libraries. The 11 outlying libraries were scheduled to close to the public on the Monday and Tuesday to allow time to change over all the peripheral set-ups and to give the staff time to re-enter all the reservations (about 2300 over the city) and have a final practice before 'going live'.

After close of business on Saturday 5 August, the telecommunications cabinet was stripped out of the University system centre and moved to the Central Library system centre. The BT engineers turned up on site on Sunday morning exactly as arranged, to move the data lines. Having already moved the exchange connections, one engineer stayed in the system centre while two others drove round the city with members of the library service's staff proving the circuits to the 11 neighbourhood libraries. That phase was completed well before lunchtime, so the rest of the day was taken up with readying Central Library's peripherals and rebuilding the cabling in the telecommunications cabinet.

On Monday morning, a technician from the modem suppliers connected their equipment to the BT lines and the stage was set for a sprint round the city setting up all the branch libraries. One person set up the small branches, while two others looked after the larger branches. Meanwhile, Central had gone live at nine o'clock on Monday morning. Something that will go down in history as the biggest non-event of the century – nothing went wrong and everything worked exactly as planned.

On Wednesday morning, 11 branches were going live at nine o'clock. We waited for the phone to ring, but it didn't – another non-event! Steve Penn, the project manager from BLCMP, arrived on site expecting at least some problems and we set off to visit all the branch libraries to check with the staff at the sharp end that all was well and that Talis and the hardware were both performing as advertised. The most difficult part of the day proved to be the decision of what we wanted to have for lunch! Twelve sites and one mobile library had gone live, and the only problems to be resolved were a few wrongly programmed function keys and a couple of recalcitrant barcode scanners.

Staff angles

The experience of installing the CLSI system had taught us that we would not be allowed (without bloodshed) the luxury of another problem-filled implementation, so we did all in our power to carry the staff with it through the change.

From the outset, staff were involved at all levels in the process of specifying and installing the new system, an action which proved very successful in that everyone who wanted to make a contribution had the opportunity to do so, engendering a feeling that they owned the new system rather than having it forced upon them. A large number of very good and helpful ideas flowed from all quarters over the months, helping the process along and contributing to the largely trouble-free implementation.

The age range of staff spans from school leavers through to those close to retirement, but all have keyboard skills and experience of an existing computer system. On the negative side, there were those who had experienced the change to CLSI and the pain it had caused and did not want to experience another change. Some who were getting close to retirement age doubted their ability to absorb a new system, and while some arranged their departures to take place prior to Talis going live, others remained, determined not to be beaten by a new computer system.

As the implementation gained momentum, weekly 'Talis User Group' meetings were introduced. The meetings were open to all levels of staff, and it was hoped that each service point would send at least one staff member. Every Friday morning at nine o'clock there was a one-hour meeting to pass on the week's news and progress. This forum was also used to make decisions on how to overcome certain problems and to find out what the staff at the sharp end wanted as regards of data input, etc. This weekly meeting was held for several weeks after going live, and was then used as a forum for sweeping up problems from both sides. It was also used on a few occasions for BLCMP's project manager to face the staff and field their questions directly. As time progressed, the meeting moved to a monthly slot and now is only convened on an 'as required' basis (roughly quarterly).

The close contact between those who were installing the system and those who would be using it was extremely valuable to both sides and worked very well. Staff attitudes to change and, in particular, changes to the computer system tend to be geographical, in that individuals can shape the views of one or more libraries both positively and negatively. The meetings and the way the staff were involved in decision-making about their computer system provided some unpredicted results. Libraries who, on their previous track record, were expected to exhibit a negative attitude shone even through adversity, while others who had previously been helpful and positive changed to uttering oaths and suchlike.

One frustrating human trait is to hearken back to previous experience. During the period of running the CLSI system, we were constantly reminded of the ancient Plessey product we had left some years before, by comments such as, 'I wish we still had Plessey, that was a much better system.' The fact that Plessey in terms of automation did very little seemed to be irrelevant, as through usage, staff had become 'comfortable' with it. Perhaps a more accurate comment would have been, 'I wish we still had Plessey, I was comfortable with that.' Right from starting work on Talis, the three people directly involved in the installation were placing bets on who would be the first to make the comment, 'I wish we still had CLSI, that was a much better system', and had even contemplated providing a large wooden spoon to reward the first individual uttering the words. Well, it wasn't a long wait. Even before the circulation system had gone live, the words were heard, but from a completely unpredicted quarter, a cataloguer who had been using Talis for about a week. The wooden spoon wasn't awarded and the phrase has only been heard a couple of times since. Perhaps that has more to do with a change in staff vocabulary towards the shorter and more succinct expressions which cannot be printed here.

Converting the staff

Talis is moduled into various 'business areas' (e.g. circulation, acquisitions and cataloguing) and training was provided along those lines. Staff numbers are such that the area which was likely to present most logistical problems for training was the most important business area: circulation.

BLCMP's training consultants provided the basics to selected members of staff, who were expected to cascade their knowledge and expertise to everyone else. There were only a few staff to be trained in working in all the non-circulation business areas. However, over 200 individuals had to be trained in circulation and over a very short period. BLCMP recommended that each staff member needed two days of training in the circulation system, which proved to be impractical in this situation. Instead, it was decided that each member of staff would receive one day of training but would also have the opportunity to use the system as much as they liked prior to the change over. In addition, a recap session was available for anyone still uncertain about any aspects of the system.

A training room was set up, which contained eight terminals to run a tutor version of Talis. An appeal for volunteers to make up the team to train the rest of the staff went out and only one person responded. The training team was to be eight strong and that was achieved by approaching members of staff who it was thought might like to do the job and who would be good at carrying it out. It was made clear that, if they did not feel comfortable with the idea, they should not take on the job. The eight people were given two days of intensive training by BLCMP staff, using some excellent documentation. Our trainers then had a week in which to get their act together and to practise on the system before starting to train the rest of the staff. The BLCMP documentation was edited down into a staff training manual, and each member of staff had a copy of their own to annotate and keep. Training took place on each week day with two trainers to eight staff members. On Saturday, one of the trainers would be on hand so that anyone who wished to use the system could come in to practise, with someone on hand to recap or answer questions. The ability to recap and practise was crucial because those staff who received their training first, turned out to have had their training three months ahead of actually going live.

Talis has its own tutor system, which duplicates the main system function-ally, and operates on a small database of about 200 title records and as many borrowers as the library may wish to input. Various training scenarios can be input into the tutor system (e.g. different kinds of reservations and borrower messages), and those scenarios can then be used in each training session and then the training database restored for the next session. The tutor system can also be used to set up and test the parameters which will be used on the main system, and the training process provided a test bed for the parameters and allowed them to be fine-tuned prior to going live. The only criticism of the tutor system was that the title records were from another Talis customer's data-base and did not mirror the way our own records would look or act on Talis. However, to be fair to BLCMP, our own records could not be used at that time because the conversion had still to take place. For future usage and testing, it is intended that the original tutor database be wiped out and that a customized database be introduced.

In any training, individual styles and personality play a large part in its suc-cess, which on BLCMP's side was very evident. We also learned some lessons on how best the training requirement should be accomplished and how differ-ent styles of presentation could complement or detract from each other. One major lesson learned was not to include the systems staff as trainers – no mat-ter how important it is that they should be expert users, their training sessions will always be interrupted by system problems, with the result that the staff who are being trained suffer.

The main system and database was available to all staff for at least one day prior to using Talis with the public and that availability played a very impor-tant part in establishing staff confidence both in themselves and in the 'beast' itself when they opened the doors on the first morning.

On the whole, while the 11 days' training provided by BLCMP as part of the contract was good and sufficient, nothing could have prepared us for dealing with such delights as UNIX, Talis parameters and MARC records. In those specific areas, a goodly quantity of 'hand holding' was required and it took some time before confidence in their use was sufficient for us to be comfortable with them.

So was it a nightmare?

A nightmare it certainly was not. A time of hard work and constant worry, it certainly was. A change to the basic operating system that a library service employs causes unrest for all concerned. If care is taken to minimize those concerns, then the actual change-over can take place quite painlessly. It takes a considerable investment of time and trouble to accomplish and, even then, improvements can always be made. The perfect system migration has yet to be achieved.

It would be easy to reflect on the past year or so, and repeat many of the trials and tribulations already mentioned. If you have read this far, you will already have a good idea of how Coventry tackled its migration and have seen edited highlights of the good and bad points in the experience. A system migration is something which does not happen very often, so it should be turned into something to enjoy not to fear. It was one of the rare occurrences in my career when I was able to accomplish a very real and lasting sense of achievement – it all worked! The celebration afterwards was very enjoyable too, what I can remember of it . . .

From our experience in Coventry, the following points should be in the forefront of the minds of those engineering a migration between computer systems:

- It has been said that 'computer salesmen are akin to those who sell used cars'.
- Remember who's paying.
- If you've checked it, get two more people to check it independently.
- Be a nuisance, keep telephoning. Let the supplier share your problems.
- Plan for every eventuality. If it can go wrong, it certainly will (Murphy's Law).
- Bravado counts for nothing, appear a fool and ask (ten times if necessary).
- Your staff matter. They do have a point of view and they do know what they are talking about, even if you don't always agree.
- The perfect computer system does not exist. It takes time to develop a good one.
- Crystal balls help, but only hard work makes a successful implementation.

Part 2: the system supplier's perspective
Steve Penn

The challenges at Coventry

All installation projects are different: so goes the project manager's 'mantra'. We like all installation projects to be different: it gives us a challenge. So my obvious starting point has to be 'What made the Coventry City Talis installation different?'

The main difference between this and my previous projects was that this was the first CLSI to Talis conversion that BLCMP had done. This meant that we were dealing with data structures and data output formats not previously encountered. However, we did have the expertise of a former CLSI employee who knew the system well.

At a high level, the conversion was fairly straightforward. The data formats were in fact quite simple and the main issue was to format the data so that it could be imported into Talis in the way that Coventry wanted. It was here that I found the first hurdle: it was easy for BLCMP staff to assess where the data should go in Talis, but it was difficult for the library service staff at Coventry to understand how their data would look in Talis. The conversion also involved matching Coventry's bibliographic data against the BLCMP database.

The process of writing the specification was quite drawn out, but we achieved it and moved into the phase of testing. Looking back it might have been better to have done a second test conversion. In fact, this is now standard BLCMP practice. The first conversion allows customers to see their data in Talis format and change their minds, the second test allows BLCMP to make sure that the process is right and to assess how long the final conversion might take to process. This was valuable experience we gained from the Coventry project.

A second test would have uncovered those instances where the input to the CLSI system had been inconsistent. Coventry searched for these in advance and found the vast majority of them. The one they didn't see and which caused some considerable difficulty for them later, was the input of a space in the borrower name. This had not been done consistently, and the result was a double sequence of borrowers in the Talis borrower index which could have been resolved at an early stage if it had been found in testing. However, as it was found at the completion of the conversion and when the system went live, we agreed that the easiest solution was online editing of the faulty borrower records.

Once the specification was agreed and the test complete, the conversion should have progressed fairly smoothly. In reality, this rarely happens and it is another reason why project management can be so challenging! Sometimes the small complications are the most difficult. In Coventry's case a significant problem arose when processing their bibliographic data from tape. The conversion had been tested with one tape and when an attempt was made to run the conversion software on the whole file, which comprised several tapes, it was found that the output format didn't include an end of tape indicator. A small problem, but as it involved a revision to the conversion software it was one that we could have done without.

Our Talis installation process is being continually improved. A great deal of time is spent planning projects and looking for things that can go wrong. This risk assessment has become more formalized and if we were doing the Coventry installation now, we would have been able to identify a serious risk with their network, although, as it happened, no problems materialized. As a result of their plan to install the Talis system centre hardware in the Central Library, as opposed to the University where their CLSI system was located, there was a requirement to change the network links to their branches over a few days, and it was not possible to test this change or reverse it if there were problems. Coventry took responsibility for this. It was planned and executed very well. Early in the project the potential risk of this part of the implementation was discussed, but circumstances meant that nothing could be done about it and that there was no point losing sleep over it! The issue was 'parked', and the weekend before the live date the changes were made. When the Central Library went live, there were no major problems with the network there. Later that week, visiting each library, it was good to find that there were no major problems at the branches either. It was enjoyable to visit the sites and to see that Talis and the Coventry staff were beginning to work well together. The last discussion on the matter between BLCMP and Coventry was a joint sigh of relief! Could it have been done any differently? Without considerable expense on Coventry's part – probably not.

Once a customer is live the next step is to get them settled down with the system, deal with the inevitable issues and questions that arise, and then end the project and hand them over to the support team. In Coventry's case this part of the process was hampered by the absence of key personnel due to sickness and other reasons. This meant that the settling down process took longer, and only some months later could they be considered to be a settled customer.

So what was learnt from the Coventry installation? The main area was in the test conversion phase, which has been improved to take account of some of the issues that Coventry raised. More generally, the Coventry experience was helpful in our general review of the installation process, which has resulted in the procedure detailed as follows.

Project management

BLCMP project management is focused to ensure successful and timely system installation. To achieve this we have found that we need to minimize surprises which could threaten the job, and we also try to help customer libraries and suppliers to meet their goals all along the line. A system installation is usually a major project for a library and BLCMP can contribute useful expertise in project management which the customer rarely has.

Figure 8.1 shows BLCMP's project management process. The process has four main stages which are discussed below:

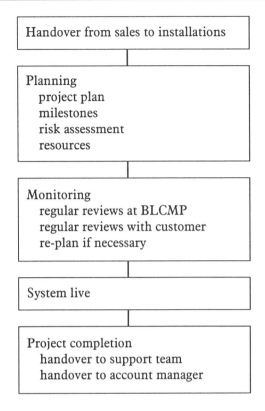

Fig. 8.1 *The installation project management process*

Planning

This is critical to a successful installation project. During this stage of the project a detailed project plan is written and all necessary resources, both at BLCMP and at the customer, are identified and committed to the project. A risk assessment is undertaken. This identifies those things that could go wrong and proposes action to be taken to minimize the risk. This can be undertaken either immediately or later in the project.

Monitoring

Monitoring a project involves

- regular reviews with the customer (normally a monthly meeting but more often as the 'go live' date draws closer) and regular contact also takes place by telephone, e-mail and fax
- a weekly review of the project at BLCMP as part of a review of all installation projects
- a monthly review by BLCMP directors of all installation projects.

At any time during a project it may be necessary to revise the plan and reschedule resources. This is done through a process of consultation and agreement with the customer. The installation is supported by installations analysts who deal with system management, functional and conversion issues.

Live date

Before going live, standard checklists are used to ensure that all necessary activity is complete. We hold the customer's hands (metaphorically speaking) throughout the period, and immediately afterwards phone every day to preempt any problems. This enables swift action to be taken and staff are poised for onsite visits if appropriate.

Project completion

As part of the project planning process, project completion criteria are agreed. Normally, a minimum of a month is allowed after go live before the project can be considered complete, but this varies from project to project and takes into account factors such as roll-out of Talis from site-to-site, and whether the data conversion is in one phase or more.

Two hand-over meetings take place: one where the project manager introduces the customer to their account manager and an internal meeting where the installations team transfer responsibility for the library to the support team. A vital part of this is having agreement on any outstanding issues and defined plans for rolling out Talis to other sites.

Conclusions

As with all such processes, project management is always evolving. All projects provide valuable experience to feed back into the installations procedure. Wherever possible, customers are given the opportunity to contribute to this by arranging a feedback session with a director. This is an open discussion which allows BLCMP to learn from the customer's experience and which builds up the spirit of cooperation which characterizes the relationship between BLCMP and its customers. Such a meeting was held with Coventry and this proved very helpful in improving the installation process. Personally, the project was enjoyable if, at times, very hectic. It was certainly a positive experience!

9 The perfect migration

Janet Broome

Introduction

Since 1993, I have been running a course for the Library Association on system migration. The final session of the course is entitled 'The perfect migration'. Many members of the library community have listened to my theories about what makes a perfect migration, but I wonder how many have put them into practice. A system migration is really about partnership, the relationship between client and supplier, I often refer to this as a marriage: the relationship has to work both ways, there needs to be a degree of flexibility and a lot of give and take.

The first part of this unusual relationship begins when the client selects the supplier which best meets their requirements for a replacement system. It is normal practice for the library to produce an operational requirement (OR) or a statement of user requirements (SOUR), which clearly states what functionality the library requires. When I produced a SOUR for Middlesex University, the final section laid the foundations of the University's expectations from the supplier with regard to day-to-day support, upgrades and training.

It is often the statement of user requirements which is referred to when suppliers do not deliver. In a perfect world and to achieve a perfect migration, this could easily be avoided if the SOUR was given an Implementation and Development sign-off before it left the supplier to be returned to the client. Having such a mechanism in place would prevent over-zealous sales people from misinterpreting the system. Librarians are worldly-wise to this and many use the SOUR to ask not only *if* the system can meet their requirements but also exactly *how* it would do so.

Contract

The statement of user requirements lays down the expectations of the client library. Elements of the SOUR may be written into the contract to protect the client library and the supplier. It is common practice among UK library automation suppliers for no work to begin on a client library without a contract being signed. The contract is there to protect both the supplier and the client library. The contract signing is the first project milestone and time should be allocated in the overall project plan for negotiations.

To take over a project where no agreed contract exists is not a desirable situation for any project manager, as more time is spent re-reading sections of unagreed contracts and referring to the original statement of user requirements than actually implementing the system. As a project manager, you can only go so far – as the terms and conditions have not been agreed, this leads to tensions and frustrations on both sides. Some librarians may believe that they are in a strong negotiating position if no contract is agreed. In my experience the contrary is true – if no contract exists and the system is half implemented there is nothing to stop the supplier from writing the project off and walking away. This has not happened in the UK, but suppliers will not be held to ransom by client libraries. When contract negotiations break down, there are moving goal posts. The contract should reflect what has been delivered, not what is about to be delivered in the future.

This is no basis for a successful working relationship. The supplier should not just be dealing with one person at the client library. A working party of one is a liability. Is this person qualified to make decisions regarding service and should this person be negotiating the contract? Most successful projects have a structure on both sides. Invariably, some systems librarians do like to take leave and they may occasionally be sick. Having more resources available at the client library does deviate some of the pressure away from the systems librarian. Library managers have an incredible gift for displaying the ostrich effect, they bury their heads in the sand and think that the system will go in no matter what – normally it is at the cost of the systems librarian's sanity.

Structured approach – steering group

The most successful migrations tend to have a senior project leader assigned to the project in addition to the systems librarian, and this person is normally the project manager for the client library. This creates an escalation path, where the project leader can make decisions in consultation with library managers regarding library policy. The systems librarian does not always have the power to make such decisions (intriguing, as it is the systems librarian who manages the library system, which helps facilitate library service and policy).

When Middlesex University went out to tender, the importance of controlling the project was realized at a very early stage. A rationale was devised whereby a series of groups was responsible for the production of the SOUR. Overall responsibility for the project was given to the Steering Group which was composed of senior managers with significant experience of system procurement and implementation in the public and academic sectors. The Steering Group really kept the project on track as Middlesex had very tight timescales. Another role of the Steering Group was to quash hidden political agendas. The biggest problem was the wording in the SOUR relating to the supply of the system. The tender was for the supply of a library system and not the supply of cataloguing records. The existing system had grown around a cataloguing cooperative – if it had been specified that the supplier must also supply bibliographic records, it would have restricted the tendering process significantly. Political agendas are a project liability and suppliers have little interest in these as they can contribute to a badly managed project. As a consultant for BDO Stoy Hayward, I was appointed to write the specification for a replacement system for a London borough. However, the systems librarian who was managing the project had different ideas about how the project should be managed, in that staff were asked to come to meetings to input into the SOUR but we were instructed not to inform staff that the system was being replaced.

Project milestones and project planning

One of the first steps for a client library when it decides to migrate is to define the project milestones. This starts with the contract signing as the first project milestone. The next step is to work back from the most important project milestone, the go-live date, to assess whether the expectations of the client library are feasible.

A system migration is a partnership and resource is required by both parties. This seems simplistic, but client libraries often underestimate how much resource is required at their end to make the project a success. This is becoming increasingly an issue with software-only deals in which more resource is required by the client library. Networks need to be ordered and implemented before the system can go live. In a client/server environment, application software needs to be loaded on each PC. Peripherals such as light pens and scanners need to be configured, in some instances these may need replacing. Printers that work on the existing system may not be compatible with the new system. All of this needs to be investigated and tested by the client library before the go-live date. In a software-only deal, the supplier is responsible for maintaining and supporting the relational database management system (RDBMS) and the application software. The supplier is not responsible for host computer operating system support, therefore the systems librarian needs to be fully conversant with the operating system, adding users, configuring printers, optimizing the kernel and devising a back-up and restore procedure. This must be tested before the site goes live.

Therefore timescales in a software-only deal need to be carefully considered and monitored. The migration process usually takes 6–8 months and there is never enough time. So, what happens when there is not enough resource at the client library? Ultimately, there are delays in the project which may have financial implications (e.g. the client library may have given their existing supplier notice on hardware and software maintenance, these agreements will need to be extended).

Project managers on the supplier side do build in contingency, but no matter how much contingency is built in to a project there is always an overwhelming factor that drives the project, the system has to go in when the new library opens, or be live for the degree show. Staffordshire University perceived the migration from Geac GLIS to Horizon as the main event the library would be involved with in summer 1995. The systems librarian had scheduled resource well, then mid-year funding was found to extend the library, this was scheduled to happen while the new system was being implemented. Again this is an issue for library managers, the migration of data from one system to another is a costly business and resourcing and commitment to the project needs to be allocated.

Once resourcing has been agreed, the project plan is issued. It is important that the project plan be reviewed and reissued at regular intervals and that regular project meetings take place at the client library.

The pre-implementation phase is the key to a successful migration. It is important that enough time be allocated to pre-implementation training and that the client library devotes enough resource to enable the systems librarian to make effective decisions regarding pre-implementation. Pre-implementation training is where all the decisions regarding the new system are made; get this wrong and the project goes pear shaped. A point made by David Jeremiah, head of computing at the National Library of Wales, is that it is people who make projects and it is people who make library automation companies. Have a bad project manager during pre-implementation and the rest of the project will be bad. It can take months if not years to move out of a bad project. Libraries should be able to choose who manages their project.

There are several approaches to pre-implementation, which have an effect on the amount of resourcing required. A common approach is to mirror the functionality from the existing system. If a library has decided to mirror functionality, it makes perfect sense for pre-implementation to take place on site at the client library. The library might want to refer to the existing system to evaluate workflows, parameters and procedures. Another option is for library managers fully to utilize the functionality of the new system and streamline some of the peculiar practices which have grown up around the existing system. Glasgow School of Art during their pre-implementation combined the techniques of mirroring the functionality on URICA and streamlining working practices. For example, the number of collection codes was reduced and materials which had the same issue policy were grouped together as one material type. It is their intention that after running with the new system they will review the modules they have implemented and plan for the implementation of reserve book room and advance booking.

A main feature of pre-implementation is agreeing what data will be converted from the existing system to the new. Most suppliers have a standard contract which contains a section on data conversions. If a library requires that acquisition and serials data be converted, this should form part of contract negotiations and be written into the standard contract. The migration of acquisition and serials data is complex, therefore more time should be allocated in the project plan for the conversion and testing of this data. There are ways round not migrating this data (e.g. the go-live date for the new system could correspond with the start of a new financial year). Most suppliers will convert bibliographic data, copy data, borrower information and some circulation transaction information.

Well-established and practised suppliers have formalized the pre-implementation process, where the client library signs off all pre-implementation decisions. This protects both the library and supplier. It is pre-implementation that enables the library to make effective decisions regarding the dataload.

Ideally, the dataload document should be written by the supplier in agreement with the client library. The reason for this is that the supplier understands the data structures of the new system, has data conversion expertise and is fully conversant with data conversion programs. Time needs to be allocated for the production of the conversion document and this requires a technical sign-off by both the supplier and the client library. It is important that members of library staff are consulted regarding the conversion. The client is led by the supplier, but it is up to the client whether to take the advice of the supplier or not. I have had experience of system managers making decisions regarding which MARC tags to convert from one system to another – when the conversion was tested in-house, all of the 690 and 691 data, which was required by the library, was lost. This is where the escalation procedure comes in. In this particular instance, the escalation path was the librarian who made the final decision regarding the data. The most valuable part of a library system is the data, it is the library's investment and needs to be protected at all costs.

A client library cannot allocate enough time to testing the data conversions. The client library must take responsibility – if the supplier asks for data to be tested, it must be tested. Discovering problems when the system has gone live may be too late.

One way of ensuring that data is checked is to perform training on the converted data. It is desirable for the client library to be trained on their own data rather than a sample training database. This enables the conversion to be checked thoroughly and assists library staff in familiarizing themselves with their data and new working procedures.

Conclusions

A perfect migration is possible if the project milestones are achievable and if the client library is realistic, there will be problems – expect problems – but there is little point at making a drama out of a minor problem. Resourcing is a key element of a successful migration, resource is needed by the client library and is also required by the supplier. One way a library can ascertain whether resources will be available for their project is by finding out how many migrations the supplier has committed resources to. Realistic timescales with contingency will go some way to alleviating the pressure at both ends. Time needs to be allocated for the testing of the data conversion and this needs to be agreed and signed off.

Further reading

John Scott Cree and Graeme Muirhead

A great deal has been written about the implementation of computerized library systems and about the management of change in libraries. This reading list only includes material which deals specifically with migration between automated systems or which seems especially relevant to the selection of a new system.

'Annual survey of automated PC- and MAC-based library system vendors', *Library systems newsletter*, **15** (5), May 1995, 41–54.

'Annual survey of automated PC- and MAC-based library system vendors', *Library systems newsletter*, **16** (5), May 1996.

Association of Research Libraries, Office of Management Services, *System migration in ARL libraries*, (SPEC kit 185), Washington, DC, ARL, 1992.

Banach, P., 'Migration from an in-house serials system to Innopac at the University of Massachusetts at Amherst', *Library software review*, **12** (1), Spring 1993, 35–7.

Barry, J., Griffiths, J.-M. and Lundeen, G., 'Automated system marketplace 1995: the changing face of automation', *Library journal*, **120** (6), 1 April 1995, 44–54.

Barry, J., Griffiths, J.-M. and Wang, P., 'Automated system marketplace for 1996: jockeying for supremacy in a networked world', *Library journal*, **121** (6), 1 April 1996, 40–51.

Barton, D. (ed.), *Making choices: the selection of library computer systems: proceedings of a seminar held at Stamford, Lincolnshire, 20th June 1996*, Capital Planning Information Ltd, 1996.

Batt, C., 'The last migration', *Public library journal*, **10** (6), November/December, 1995, 159–61.

Berry, J., 'Upgrading systems, software, and microcomputers', *Library journal*, 15 September 1989, 56–9.

Blunden-Ellis, J. and Graham, M. E., 'A UK market survey of library automation system vendors (1992–1993)', *Program*, **28** (2), April 1994, 109–24.

Boss, R. W., 'Client/server technology for libraries with a survey of offerings', *Library technology reports*, **30** (6), November–December 1994, 681–744.

Boss, R. W., 'Online catalog functionality in the 90s: vendor responses to a model RFP', *Library technology reports*, **29** (5), September–October 1993, 587–745.

Boss, R. W., 'The procurement of library automated systems', *Library technology reports*, **26** (5), September–October 1990, 629–749.

Boss, R. W. and Casey, M. H., 'Operating systems for automated library systems', *Library technology reports*, **27** (2), March–April 1991, 181–3.

Boyd, W. A., 'Trends in library automation', *Georgia librarian*, **31** (3), Fall 1994, 59–62.

Briscoe, G., 'Migration: a natural growth process for libraries (part one of two)', *Trends in law library management and technology*, **6** (7), March 1995, 1–3.

Briscoe, G., 'Migration: a natural growth process for libraries (part two of two)', *Trends in law library management and technology*, **6** (8), April 1995, 4–6.

Broome, J., 'Market influences and the role of the systems librarian', in Muirhead, G. (ed.), *The systems librarian: the role of the library systems manager*, London, Library Association Publishing, 1994.

Carson, S. M., 'Library Information Access System at the Pennsylvania State University: a migration story', in Head, J. W. and McCabe, G. B. (eds.), *Insider's guide to library automation in practical experience*, Westport, Conn., Greenwood, 1993, 31–42.

Casale, M., 'Know your systems', *Library manager*, March 1996, 21–3.

Cervarich, C. S., 'System migration: a bibliographic essay', in Head, J. W. and McCabe, G. B. (eds.), *Introducing and managing academic library automation projects*, Greenwood, 1996.

Cibarelli, P., 'Library automation alternatives in 1996 and user satisfaction ratings of library users by operating system', *Computers in libraries*, **16** (2), February 1996, 26–35.

Cortez, E. M., *Proposals and contracts for library automation: guidelines for preparing RFPs*, Studio City, Pacific Information Inc., 1987.

Cortez, E. M. and Smorch, T., *Planning second generation automated library systems*, Greenwood, 1993.

Dye, J., 'DYNIX to LIBERTAS: the management of change', *VINE*, **83**, August 1991, 10–18.

Epstein, S. B., 'Implementing a second system: some new concerns', *Library journal*, **116** (1), January 1991, 77.

Epstein, S. B., 'Second-time library system buyers: differing realities, differing expectations', *Library journal*, **115** (21), December 1990, 100–1.

Epstein, S. B., 'Testing: did you get what you bought?', *Library journal*, **110** (8), 1 May 1985, 34.

Gozzi, T., Pfeiffer, C., and Somers, M., 'The great migration: choosing our next system', *ALCTS news*, **12** (22), 27 January 1997. Internet WWW page at URL: ftp://ftp.lib.ncsu.edu/stacks/a/ann/ann-v12n22.txt (version current at 24 February 1997).

Hallmark, J. and Garcia, C. R., 'System migration: experiences from the field', *Information technology and libraries*, **11** (4), 1992, 345–58.

Hamilton, M. J., 'The great migration: second generation acquisition and library management systems', *Acquisitions librarian*, **13/14**, 1995, 5–33.

Harrison, D. and Favret, L., 'London Borough of Bromley: from ALS to Geac in six months', *VINE*, 75, October 1989, 4–7.

Heath, B., 'Migrating between online acquisitions systems: organizing information and staff', *Acquisitions librarian*, 12, 1994, 15–26.

Hegarty, K., 'Vendor abandonment', *Library journal*, 111 (2), 1 February 1986, 47.

Hentz, M. B., 'Data conversion from FAXONS SC-10 serials control system into Techlib-Plus (R) online card catalog', *Special libraries*, 89 (3), 1995, 162–82.

Heseltine, R., 'Choosing in the dark: strategic issues in the selection of library automation systems', *ITs news*, 27, April 1993, 13–18.

Heseltine, R., 'New directions in the library automation industry: the prospects for structural change', in *Computers in libraries international 93: proceedings of the seventh annual Computers in libraries conference held in London in February 1993*, 125–9.

Heseltine, R., 'New perspectives on library management systems: a Pilgrim's Progress', *Program*, 28 (1) January 1994, 53–61.

Hewitt, J. A. (ed.), *Advances in library automation and networking*, Vol. 6, JAI Press, 1996.

Huang, J. L. and Ting, Z., 'Migration from LS/2000 to KeyNOTIS: a medium-sized academic library's experience', *Information technology and libraries*, 14 (3), September 1995, 185 (5).

'International survey of automated library system vendors: integrated multi-user multi-function systems running on mainframes, minis, and micros that use a multi-user operating system', *Library systems newsletter*, 15 (3 and 4), March and April 1995, 17–39.

'International survey of automated library system vendors: integrated multi-user multi-function systems running on mainframes, minis, and micros that use a multi-user operating system', *Library systems newsletter*, 16 (3 and 4), March and April 1996, 17–32.

Jacob, W., 'System migration: bettering tomorrow today', in *IOLS '91: integrated online library systems: proceedings – 1991, New York, May 8–9, 1991*, Learned Information, 1991, 65–72.

Jasper, R. P., 'Systems migration', *ACQNET*, 2 (100), 28 October 1992. Internet WWW page at URL: ftp://ftp.lib.ncsu.edu/pub/stacks/acq/acq-v2n100 (version current at 24 February 1997).

Jordin, A., 'Changing a centralised library automation system', in *Computers in libraries international '91: proceedings of the 5th annual computers in libraries, London, February 1991*, London, Meckler, 1991, 13–16.

Keller, P., 'Notes on migration from LS/2000 to NOTIS or another system', *Lines of support*, Fall 1992, 3–5.

Kington, R. A., 'Responding to an RFP: a vendor's viewpoint', *Library hi-tech*, 5 (1), Spring 1987, 61–5.

Klobas, J. E., 'Managing technological change in libraries and information services', *The electronic library*, 8 (5), October 1990, 344–9.

Kneedler, W. H., 'The Phoenix Public Library migration. Part 1: the birth and death of an early system', *Online libraries and microcomputers*, **6** (11), November 1988, 1–5.

Kneedler, W. H., 'The Phoenix Public Library migration. Part 2: selecting a new system, migration', *Online libraries and microcomputers*, **6** (12), December 1988, 1–11.

Knoblauch, C. J., 'Automating the library: take two', in *IOLS '90: integrated online library systems: proceedings – 1990, New York, May 2–3, 1990*, Medford, N.J., Learned Information, 1990, 115–20.

Lambert, A., *Online system migration guide*, American Library Association, 1996.

Lee, C., 'The vendor's corner—the Request for Proposal', *Library hi-tech*, **5** (1), Spring 1987, 91.

Leeves, J., *Library management systems: current market and future prospects: a report prepared for the SCONUL Advisory Committee on Information Systems*, London, SCONUL, 1995.

Library Information Technology Centre, *Guide to choosing an automated library system*, British Library Board, 1992, (LITC Report number 2).

Lloyd-Williams, M. and Grant, H., 'System migration in an academic library: an intra-vendor experience', *New review of information and library research*, **1**, 1995, 39–56.

Martin, M., 'Financing library automation: selling benefits and the budget', *Bottom line*, charter issue, 1989, 15.

Matthews, J., 'Moving to the next generation: Aston University's selection and implementation of Galaxy 2000', *VINE*, **10**, December 1995, 42–9.

Matthews, J. R., Salmon, S. R. and Williams, J. F., 'The RFP – Request for Punishment: or a tool for selecting an automated library system', *Library hi-tech*, **5** (1), spring 1987, 17.

Michael, J., 'Risky business: financial viability of systems vendors', *Library hi-tech*, **5** (3), Fall 1987, 110.

Michael, J. J., 'The vendor's corner—the Request for Proposal', *Library hi-tech*, **5** (1), Spring 1987, 95.

Muir, S. P., 'Selecting and installing a second system', in Head, J. W. and McCabe, G. B. (eds.), *Insider's guide to library automation in practical experience*, Greenwood, 1993, 65–85.

Pachent, G., 'Network 95: choosing a third generation automated information system for Suffolk Libraries & Heritage', *Program*, **30** (3), July 1996, 213–28.

Perley, D. R., *Implementing open systems*, London, McGraw-Hill, 1995.

Perley, D. R., *Migrating to open systems: taming the tiger*, London, McGraw-Hill, 1993.

Pitkin, G. M. (ed.), *Library systems migration: changing automated systems in libraries and information centers*, Meckler, 1991.

Pourciau, L. J., 'Automated library system migration in the United States', *The electronic library*, **10** (2), 1992, 103–8.

Pourciau, L. J., 'Satisfaction and dissatisfaction with IOLS hardware', in *IOLS*

'91: integrated online library systems: proceedings – 1991, NewYork, May 8–9, 1991, Learned Information, 1991, 123–30.

Rush, J., 'The consultant's corner – the RFP in the automation procurement process', *Library hi-tech*, 5 (1), Spring 1987, 104.

Rush, J., 'The library automation market: why do vendors fail? A history of vendors and their characteristics', *Library hi-tech*, 6 (3), 1988, 7–33.

Saffady, W., 'Integrated library systems for minicomputers and mainframes: a vendor study', Part 1, *Library technology reports*, 30 (1), January–February 1994, 1–150.

Saffady, W., 'Integrated library systems for minicomputers and mainframes: a vendor study', Part 2, *Library technology reports*, 30 (2), March–April 1994, 155–323.

Schappert, C. H., 'The library automation project: is it ever really done?', in Head, J. W. and McCabe, G. B. (eds.), *Insider's guide to library automation in practical experience*, Greenwood, 1993, 261–71.

Schwarz, P. T., 'Selection of an automated library system for the University of Wisconsin cluster libraries', *Information technology and libraries*, March 1987, 40–56.

Seaman, S., 'Circulation data migration: a CARL Systems to Innovative Interfaces case study', *LIBRES: library and information science research electronic journal*, 6 (1 and 2), June 1996. Internet WWW page at URL: http://www.lib.ncsu.edu/stacks/libres/libres-v6n1-2.html (version current at 24 February 1997).

Sessions, J. and Post, W., 'Moving from a first generation to a second generation online catalog database', in *Energies for transition*, Chicago Association of College and Research Libraries, American Library Association, 1986, 236–8.

Silva, J., 'The selection and implementation of integrated automated systems in Victorian public libraries', in McMullin, B. J. and Rasmussen, R. (eds.), *Proceedings of the Public Library Research Forum: public librarianship: a critical nexus, Monash University, 8 April 1994*, Ancora, 1995, 67–80.

Simon, A. R. *System migration: a complete reference*, Van Nos Rheinhold, 1993.

Smith, B. G. and Borgendale, M. 'The second time around: the next generation local online system', *Library journal*, July 1988, 47–51.

Stevens, P., 'Migrating from one online acquisitions system to another', *ACQNET*, 1 (99), 28 August 1991. Internet WWW page at URL: ftp://ftp.lib.ncsu.edu/pub/stacks/acq/acq-v1n099 (version current at 24 February 1997).

Sylge, C. 'Cautious progress: library automation systems in the '90s', *Managing information*, 7/8, July/August 1995, 22–5.

Tedd, L. A., 'Computer-based library systems: a review of the last twenty-one years', *Journal of documentation*, June 1987, 145–65.

Valauskas, E. J., 'Avoiding fossilization: migrating information between databases', *Database*, 15 (3), June 1992, 94–5.

Vendor failure', *Library systems newsletter*, 9 (10), October 1989, 76.

Wan, W. W., 'System migration and its impact on technical services', *Public library quarterly*, **13** (4), 1993, 13–20.

Wang, S. S., 'MIT libraries Barton replacement on hold'. Internet WWW page at URL: http://the-tech.mit.edu/V114/N43/library.43n.html (version current at 25 November 1996).

Wanninger, P. D., 'The sound and the fury of RFP', *Library journal*, **115** (21), December 1990, 87–9.

Whittaker, D., 'The Essex problem: how Essex migrated from an offline to an online system', *VINE*, **92**, September 1993, 28–35.

Williams, J. F., 'The RFI, RFP, RFQ and contract process', in Cargill, J. (ed.), *Integrated online library catalogs*, (Supplements to Computers in libraries; 21), Westport, Meckler, 1991, 1–16.

Wilson, M., 'Talis at Nene: an experience in migration in a college library', *Program*, **28** (3), July 1994, 239–51.

Index